HAPPINESS STRATEGY

STRATEGY AND HAPPINESS FOR EVERYONE

Rajesh K Pillania

PhD (Strategy)

Invincible Publishers

First Printing: 2020

ISBN: 978-93-89600-17-9

Invincible Publishers

Registered Address: 201A, SAS Tower, Sector 38, Gurgaon - 122003

This book is dedicated to
my parents
who taught me the most important lessons in happiness.

Disclaimer

This book is a work of fiction and any resemblance with any individual, organization, situation, event, or work is a mere coincidence and the author bears no responsibility for the same.

This book is written in a lighter vein and it doesn't intend to hurt anyone's sentiments or emotions.

Praise for Happiness Strategy

"Most unique and humorous way to learn about basics of strategy and its application for generating personal happiness. Happiness Strategy makes learning a boring subject very enjoyable. My own happiness went up after reading this book. Buy it and you will like it."

Jagdish N. Sheth, Charles Kellstadt Professor of Business, Goizueta Business School, Emory University, USA.

"Happiness is beautifully brought about by "Happiness Strategy". A must read."

Sir Dr. Huzaifa Khorakiwala. CEO, Wockhardt Foundation.

"At its essence, strategy is largely structured and intelligent thinking. However, the way it is taught in class – with the same old complex definitions and models – often makes it drab and boring. Prof. Pillania's initiative then to simplify strategy using fun anecdotes is a welcome change. And the parallel theme of finding the philosophy of happiness makes it absolutely scintillating."

Mr. Nishant Saxena, Global Chief Strategy Officer, Cipla.

"The word strategy is plagued with the misfortune of evoking complex images in our minds. Consequently, it is a concept that has become a denizen of hallowed halls and a concept that is considered to be of little relevance in the life of the common man. 'Happiness Strategy' elegantly drives home the error of this belief and very simply demonstrates how the basic tenets of strategy can be incorporated to improve quality of everyday life.

An insightful read for both, the formal practitioners of strategy as well as the common man."

Mr. Alok Sinha, Chief Strategy Officer, Initiative.

"It is light, humorous, deliberately simple and the idea of associating strategy and the quest for happiness worked for me. Great job!"

Mr. Ram Gopal, CEO, Barclays Bank India.

"If you want to have fun while learning strategy, this is the right book for you! I love the way Professor Pillania uses stories and vivid examples to make strategy easy."

Professor Jochen Wirtz, Vice Dean Graduate Studies, NUS Business School, National University of Singapore.

"Business strategy, much like happiness, is widely perceived as elusive and, occasionally, elitist. In reality, the best practices that comprise effective corporate strategy are surprisingly simple and relatable, as 'Happiness Strategy' affirms. I would highly recommend the book as an easy-to-grasp yet insightful read, covering strategy principles that are equally relevant in our professional and personal lives."

Ms. Sangeeta Prasad, CEO and Managing Director, Mahindra Lifespace Developers Ltd.

"Another accessible book having nuggets of knowledge by Dr. Rajesh Pillania, a prolific researcher and professor of strategy. His efforts to simplify the challenging subject of strategy are laudable. The book introduces useful concepts of strategy through daily life situations a learner faces. Very affordable way to learn the basics of happiness strategy. Implement some ideas to initiate your journey of happiness!"

Dr. Kirankumar S. Momaya,
Professor, SJM School of Management, IIT Bombay &
President, Global Institute of Flexible Systems
Management (GIFT).

Other Humorous Books by the Same Author

Strategic Humour: Democratizing Strategy

Love Strategy: A New Perspective on Love, Relationships, Life and Strategy.

Startup Humor: Democratizing Startup Strategy

Forthcoming Book:

Learning Strategy in Fun way with The Big Bang Theory

Book with a Social Cause

All royalties earned from this book will be donated to the cause of education.

Table of Contents

Acknowledgment

This book wouldn't have been possible without support from number of people.

I am grateful to Professor B. Bhattacharyya, Former Dean IIFT; Professor T. N. Kapoor, Founder Director, MDI; Prof Satish Kapoor, Former Chairperson, UBS, Punjab University; Prof. Prem Vrat, Formerly Director, IIT Roorkee and Director-in-charge, IIT Delhi; and Professor Akbar, Former Dean & Professor IIM, Lucknow for their encouragement. I am grateful to Professor Kirankumar S Momaya, IIT Mumbai for his valuable inputs, and Professor Sushil, IIT Delhi for his encouragement for this book.

I am thankful to my colleagues at MDI namely Professor Ashok Panjwani, Professor Manoj Anand, Dr. Anthony Jose, Librarian and Professor Ankur Roy; and FPM scholar Nupur for reading the manuscript and giving their valuable insights for improving the book. I am grateful to my students Tariq, Aayush and Yamini and colleagues at MDI namely Professors Shaphali, Anshul, and Nukul for sharing interesting insights.

I am thankful to Ms. Dearbhla O'Reilly for proofreading the manuscript and her critical inputs for improving the manuscript.

I have observed and heard over the years' a number of funny incidences of MBA life from friends and students and acknowledge them all here and I am grateful for their inputs.

Last, but not the least, I acknowledge the strategy professors who have coined various strategy concepts over the years which are explained in this book.

Preface

There are a lot of similarities between the concepts of strategy and happiness. Strategy is one of the most widely misunderstood and misused words in the business world. It is made to appear as a very complicated and done-to-death boring topic; and, as if it is relevant only for top management. This is not good for the desired results from the strategy domain and for strategy itself. Similar to strategy, happiness is made to appear a very difficult and ivory tower topic. Almost everyone wants happiness and there has been a search for happiness for a very long time. There are numerous people dreaming of bliss and nirvana one day but doing nothing much about it.

The primary purpose of this book is to explain strategy in a simple, fun, and applicable way. It uses the context of happiness to explain strategy concepts for the masses. There are very few people with access to formal business education and even in business schools strategy is made to appear as a very difficult and boring subject.

The secondary purpose of the book is to make happiness easy for everyone. This book defines happiness in a simple way. It makes it easy for everyone to bring happiness to their lives with the help of strategy concepts.

Happiness Masterclass 1

Keep it simple and fun. Smile ☺

The best things and strategies are so simple that they look so obvious in hindsight!

Start and end your day with a smile. It is easy.

Part I

The Beer Party Plan

ABBC is among the top management schools in the country. One of its programs is a one year executive MBA which is for people who have worked for some time in the industry. There are sixty students and they come from different backgrounds, with varied experiences, from different age groups, and from various parts of the country. There are a few international students also in the program.

It is the first class of the first day of the program. Students are entering the class room, taking their places and talking casually. A guy named Ravi enters and goes to the last row and sits there. Ravi starts talking to the two other students, Ekta and Eva, in the same last row and suggests maybe they should move to the first row. Ekta and Eva tell Ravi that they are taking the last row because it has many advantages such as they can just chill or chit chat or use their mobile phone once in a while. They tell Ravi it is a big class room and rows are in ascending size, so the Professor can't figure out what are we doing in the last row. Ravi agrees with them and then the bell rings for the lecture. At that moment, Ravi takes the podium.

Ravi: Good morning.

Class responds by saying good morning.

I am Professor Ravi and I am your faculty for the basics of management course.

Ekta and Eva look very taken back and embarrassed.

Ravi: Today I learned the advantages of being in the last row in the class, from two of your friends (*points towards Ekta and Eva*).

Ekta and Eva look very embarrassed.

The class bursts out in laughter.

Ravi: So thanks to them, I am going to give my very special attention to the last row.

The class again laughs.

The session continues.

*****

It's the third day in the executive MBA program and the program office sends an email in which groups for project works are announced.

Nitish, Surender, Manoj, Eva, Ekta and Varun are in one group for project work.

Nitish is 27 year old and has high expectations. He is thinking of making the best use of his abilities and resources to reach the top and go places.

Brigadier Surender is a retired army officer, 58 years old and thinking of spending the rest of his life exploring spirituality and religion. He is thinking maybe he can get some management ideas to better his way to spirituality and religion. Maybe he wants to join some religious or spiritual organization and devote a big part of his remaining days to that organization.

Manoj is a corporate executive, 42 years old who has suffered a second heart attack last year and is thinking of finding his way in life.

Ekta is 34 years old and got divorced recently and is still not over it. She has compromised on her career over the years for marriage. She wants to get a fresh start to her professional life.

Eva is 51 years old. She has spent her life on raising kids and professional success. She has been lamenting on not doing much philanthropy from the last few years. She wants to start something philanthropic and she is thinking this management program is going to help her in putting her ideas into practice.

Varun is 31 years old and has failed multiple times in startups after leaving a high paying job. He is looking for a more settled corporate life.

It has been very hectic first three days on campus. Students are still figuring out their way. Ekta suggests the group to go for a beer party on Friday evening in Downtown, Sector 29, Gurgaon. It will be a nice ice breaker for the group. She belongs to Gurgaon and knows the city inside out. Everybody agrees to it.

*****

Happiness Masterclass 2

Identify the meaning of happiness for you.

Happiness is inside of you, and it is not in comparison to anyone else.

Happiness is now. Accept the way things are. Then work to change them if you want.

Part II

What Is Happiness?

Friday evening in Downtown, Sector 29, Gurgaon.

Varun: It is a cool place! I like it.

Others also agree.

After settling down and after two drinks.

Brigadier Surender: I have seen life and done almost everything. What is bothering me these days is that I have not explored religion or spirituality at all and I feel so empty inside at times. All my life I was so busy with so many things that I could not find time for religion and spirituality. Now I am retired and don't know how many more years are left and it makes me so unhappy that I just ignored this part so much. And I feel more so after I lost my wife a few months ago.

Manoj: Oh My God, That's so terrible. But look at positives boss, at least you are in good health. I had a second heart attack last year and that scared the hell out of me. I have two small kids to take care of and a wonderful wife, to whom I have not given much time. In the corporate rat race I ignored my health and now it looks like health has left me for good!

Ekta: Oh that's really sad! But you are lucky that you have a wonderful wife and two kids. It is so nice that you care so much for your family. Look at me, I married an idiot under family pressure and spoiled my life.

Eva: You poor girl! I feel so sorry for you. It must be terrible for you.... Sadly, I am also fighting my own demons...I see so many problems in our society, so many poor small kids on streets but I have not done anything for them and that is not letting me sleep for the last few years!

Varun: Great, that's a noble idea to help others. But I am a bit selfish and I am not able to help myself, forget about helping others! I am a big failure and three of my startups have just failed miserably and I have lost whatever I have earned! I have taken a bank loan to finance this MBA program.

Nitish: All...All of you have gone through a lot! That's so painful. I am just starting my life and let's see where I mess up!

Ekta: Please don't mess it my way at least!

On the way back to the institute, Nitish starts thinking that he doesn't want to be unhappy like any of these five people and needs to find some way to avoid this sadness and find a way to be happy.

*****

Next day, in the strategy class.

It is the first day of strategy class.

Professor: We are going to start with an important strategy exercise. Please raise your right hand.

Students raise their right hand.

Professor: Now with this hand pull the left ear of student sitting next to you.

The students look confused but pull the left ear of student sitting next to them.

Professor: (*With a smile*) This is strategy!

Students look a bit amused first and then laugh out loud.

Professor: (*With a smile*) Well, I cannot pull your ears, so I have outsourced this part to you!

Students laugh out loud.

Professor: On a serious note, this is one of the big problems with strategy. Almost everyone claims to be a strategy expert and says anything in the name of strategy.

And the class continues.

In the afternoon, after classes, Nitish meets his strategy Professor Husmukh Doordarshi.

Nitish: You have suggested that we will gain the maximum from strategy if we apply it on ourselves first. Is it really possible?

Professor Doordarshi: Yes, it is definitely possible.

Nitish: Oh, ok. In that case, is it possible to make a strategy for happiness for myself?

Professor Doordarshi: That's interesting. And very important too. But first you need to help me. Tell me what do you mean by "Being Happy".

Nitish: I am not sure about what I mean by being happy.

Professor Doordarshi: That's the big problem. Almost everyone wants to be happy but they don't know what they mean by happiness. Excuse me, I need to complete this email and then need to call someone.

It will take couple of minutes. Till then you ask yourself this question and find an answer for me.

Nitish: Oh! Ok.

Professor Doordarshi: Oh! You look confused. What's wrong with the world! Everyone wants a quick fix, at least you don't fall in that trap. The 'art of asking questions' is losing steam in business schools. This is a fundamental skill MBA students need to have, but sadly it is not given that much importance in business schools.

Nitish: I agree.

And Professor Doordarshi goes back to completing the email he was writing when Nitish entered his office.

> Art of Asking Questions
>
> Art of Asking Questions: To find the solution to any problem, it is very important to ask good questions and it is an art that can be learned with practice.
>
> Application in the story: Nitish is more focused on jumping to solving his problem and not on asking good questions to understand the problem.
>
> It's your turn now: Do you ask good questions to understand Happiness? What are your questions? What should they be?

*****

After 5 minutes.

Professor Doordarshi: What have you figured out by now?

Nitish: I am trying hard.

Professor Doordarshi: You need to think and tell me what you mean by being happy and only then I can help you. You need to first answer this question. Strategy is for the long term and you need to think like that.

Nitish: I want to enjoy life.

Professor Doordarshi: So enjoying life is what you mean by happiness.

Nitish: I guess; I mean I don't want to live an unhappy life.

Professor Doordarshi: Tell me what can make you unhappy?

Nitish: Oh yes, yesterday I was with some of my classmates and they shared their stories. And I don't want to end up being unhappy like them.

Professor Doordarshi: What is wrong with you? If you want to be happy, you need to stop comparing yourself with others. Comparison with others is a sure way to stay unhappy for rest of your life.

Nitish: Yes, I agree.

Professor Doordarshi: But you can learn from others. So what are your learnings from listening to their stories?

Nitish: Oh, yes. From listening to their stories, I gathered that I don't want to be professionally unsuccessful, have broken personal relationships, health challenges, fear of not doing enough philanthropy for society; and frustration of not connecting with spirituality/religion.

Professor Doordarshi: Yes, that's good. So based on what you shared, let's say there are 5 Dimensions of Happiness. And these are to be professionally successful, have good personal relationships, good health, make contributions through philanthropy and connecting with spirituality/religion. Let's call it 'Minimum viable happiness' which means lack of stress due to any major trouble in the five areas of life namely, professional success, personal relationships, health, philanthropy, and spirituality/religion.

Nitish: Yes, that would make me happy, I guess.

Professor Doordarshi: Yes, it is a good start. Unfortunately, the world keeps dreaming of achieving 'Bliss' or 'Nirvana' but does nothing about it, and keeps postponing to go after it some day in future. Which is a lost cause. So I like this idea of keeping it simple and it is doable for majority of us.

Professor Doordarshi: So you want to be happy once and got done with it?

Nitish: I want to be happy and stay happy.

Professor Doordarshi: In that case you need to take care of these five dimensions not once but continuously.

Nitish: Yes, I agree.

Professor Doordarshi: And then you will be enjoying life?

Nitish: Yes, if I am not unhappy but happy with myself then I am enjoying life.

Professor Doordarshi: Good. So now you have some working definition of happiness. Now go and apply your knowledge of strategy and come back if you have any doubts.

Nitish: Yes, that seems to be a good approach. I didn't think about it that way.

Professor Doordarshi: This is the problem of your generation. You don't know the destination but are in hurry to hit the road! You are more focused on the solution part. That's the wrong approach. First you need to define the problem. Once it is well defined, it is easy to solve it. And to well define a problem, you need to ask questions. This art of framing a problem needs to be taught more in the business schools.

Nitish: I can't agree more. Thank you, Professor Husmukh Doordarshi.

Art of Framing a Problem

Art of Framing a Problem: It means identifying and describing a problem correctly.

Application in the story: Nitish is more focused on jumping to solving his problem and not on framing the problem.

It's your turn now: How are you framing your problem of Happiness? Is it correct? What should it be?

*****

After a couple of days, in the night, Nitish is not able to sleep and his mind goes wandering.

I am feeling lost in this program. The focus of students seem to be more on placements than academics and the placement committee dictates the terms here. They are treating us as inventory which needs to be sold to companies! I am not sure it is same as I expected. I don't know how it is going to unfold.

I should stop thinking about it. I think I will be able to survive here. Let's think of the positive side and work on my strategy.

It is very helpful to apply concepts of strategy on myself assuming I am CEO of myself. But it is so maddeningly difficult to apply it on happiness for myself. And that too when it has Five Dimensions! It is easier said than done. I am not sure how to go about it. Left to me alone, I will never be able to make it.

What is the way out? Should I ask my elder sister, but she knows nothing?

Should I ask my school time friend, but when I am finding it difficult, what would he know about it?

Maybe I should ask my father, but he will beat me up!

Should I ask my mother, but she will think I am on drugs?

What If I ask my classmates here, but they might make fun of me?

But I can ask my project group members, they seem to be nice people. Maybe they are one option.

Or I go back to strategy Professor Doordarshi and seek his help? Yes, that seems a good idea but I can't share all information with him and can't take too much of his time. Then what to do?

Let me think about it tomorrow. It's already 3am. Need to catch at least few hours of sleep and get up on time for the morning class. If I get late even by one minute for the class, the crazy Professor will ask me to keep standing with him for the rest of the lecture!

*****

Next day, in the strategy class.

At the end of the session, the Professor is taking attendance.

A guy with heavy manly voice makes proxy attendance for a girl student!

The Professor pauses for a moment.

Professor: "Seriously? You should know there is a difference in a female and a male voice!"

The class laughs out loud.

The Professor also busts out in laughter.

In the afternoon, in the strategy Professor Husmukh Doordarshi's office.

Nitish: Thank you for giving me your time Professor Husmukh Doordarshi.

Professor Doordarshi: That's all right. Tell me what progress you have made.

Nitish: I am totally lost. If you ask me to apply strategy concepts on myself assuming I am CEO of myself, I can do a bit of it. But to apply strategy for happiness on all five dimensions of happiness, looks so overwhelming.

Professor Doordarshi: You need to learn how to solve complex problems. One of the ways to deal with a complex problem is to break it into parts and then deal with one part at a time. This makes it relatively less complex and doable. Unfortunately, this 'art of structured thinking' is also not taught properly in business schools. For your problem, break strategy into four parts of developing strategic intent, formulating strategy, implementing strategy, and evaluation and feedback.

Nitish: Yes, I think that is a great way. Let me try and apply strategy concepts in this way on happiness.

Professor Doordarshi: Good. First go and work on the first part of it, i.e. go and get your intent right.

Nitish: Yes, I am on it now.

Professor Doordarshi: Ok go and keep trying and come back only when you have penned down your thoughts on what we have discussed. You need to show me some real progress through some good home work next time rather than making castles in the air.

Nitish: Yes, sir.

Art of Structured Thinking

Art of Structured Thinking: To find the solution to any complex problem, it is very important to think in a structured way and break it into parts and then deal with one part at a time.

Application in the story: Nitish is overwhelmed with the complexity of the problem and Professor Doordarshi suggests him to think in a structured way and break the problem into parts and then solve it. This is structured thinking.

It's your turn now: Do you apply structured thinking for Happiness? Do you think, it is correct? What should it be?

*****

Happiness Masterclass 3

Find a meaning to your life.

Every happy soul has found a meaning to its existence. The meaning need not be a very grand or ambitious one. It should be what makes sense to you.

If you are not able to find a purpose or meaning to your life, don't worry. Till you find it, you can create happiness through small acts of kindness for others.

Part III

Setting The Intent Right

That night after everyone has gone to bed.

Nitish thinks why not have a happiness vision for him to take care of this issue head-on, and work only on first dimension to start with. So he develops an overall happiness vision and one for first dimension of happiness.

Happiness Vision: To be and stay a happy person.

[By taking care of all five dimensions of happiness i.e. be professionally successful, have meaningful personal relationships, have good health, engage in philanthropy and take care of spirituality/religion.]

And from this I can draw a vision for each part of my life. For example, for the professional part of my life, my vision can be.

Professional Success Vision: To be a successful corporate professional.

Vision

Vision: Vision is what an organization aspires to be in the future. It should be a guiding and motivating force that is neither impossible to achieve nor easily attainable. It should be clear, brief and memorable.

Application in the story: To be and stay a happy person. This is called vision.

It's your turn now: Do you have a vision for Happiness? What is it? What should it be?

*****

Nitish gets excited with the clarity he got starting with the vision. He puts it on paper and realizes it helps in thinking more clearly.

It is not as difficult as I was thinking. And putting it on paper really helps. I can also make my mission for happiness. And it can be as follows:

Happiness Mission: While being happy, to contribute in whatsoever small way to the happiness of the world.

And from this I can draw a mission for each part of my life. For example, for the professional part of my life, my mission can be.

Professional Success Mission: While being successful, to contribute to the success of the corporate sector and its various stakeholders.

Mission

Mission: Mission means the core purpose of an organization. It justifies the organization's existence. It should be clear, brief and memorable.

Application in the story: His mission is while being happy, to contribute in whatsoever small way to the happiness of the world.

It's your turn now: Do you have a mission for Happiness? What is it? What should it be?

*****

Nitish finds himself on a roll and continues.

I am going great. It is fun. Now I can also create my core values for happiness.

Happiness Core Values: Respect, love and care for fellow human beings and the larger universe.

And from this I can draw core values for each part of my life. For example, for professional part of my life, my core values can be as follows.

Professional Success core values: To be a dedicated and committed professional with respect, care and love for others.

Core Values

Core Values: Core values are the core principles of the organization which are deep rooted in the organization, define its culture, bind its people together and cannot be compromised for short term benefits or convenience.

Application in this story: Respect, love and care for fellow human beings and the larger universe.

It's your turn now: What are your core values? What should they be? Do your core values come in the way for finding Happiness?

*****

Next day, in the strategy class.

The Professor is sharing his thoughts on innovation strategy but he suddenly stops and is staring at Varun who appears to be taking a nap.

Varun is woken up by the silence and sees the Professor staring at him.

Varun: I was not sleeping. I was concentrating with closed eyes.

The class laughs out loud.

Professor: (*After laughing out loudly*) Thanks for being so considerate, but I never thought it requires so much of deep concentration or going into a trance!

The class laughs out loud.

In the afternoon, in the office of Professor Doordarshi.

Nitish: I was finding it difficult to apply strategy on happiness.

Professor Doordarshi: Who told you it is going to be a piece of cake? It is difficult in the beginning.

Nitish: Yes, it is difficult. But last night, I was able to think through it, and came up with good results for vision, mission and core values. Here are these I have written for your feedback.

Professor Doordarshi: That's a good beginning. Was it as difficult as you were thinking?

Nitish: Yes, Professor it was not that difficult as my thoughts became much clearer once I started putting them on paper. I am going to follow your advice. It works.

Professor Doordarshi: You are making good progress. Keep going. But it is going to be much more difficult from now onwards, particularly when you are going to use various frameworks.

Nitish: Yes, that is scary.

Professor Doordarshi: Don't be scared. You need to be happy from now onwards as your vision is to be happy and stay happy. Don't get bothered by the future problems today. You deal with them head- on when they arrive. You be ready and prepared for them but don't unnecessarily worry about them.

Nitish: Yes, I need to follow the vision otherwise it is of no use as you said in the lecture. I need to look for solutions for the complexities I am going to face while going forward on this happiness journey.

Professor Doordarshi: Good. And yes engage your friends in this to get their help and insights too.

Nitish: Yes, that's how I am going to proceed. Thanks Professor for your time.

*****

Happiness Masterclass 4

Tap into the unlimited possibilities with the power of positive energy and thoughts.

Life is full of unimaginable possibilities for those who are full of positivity.

Stay positive, surround yourself with positive people and tap into positive energy of the universe.

Part IV

The Path To Happiness

(Strategy Formulation)

It is Friday evening and the group meets again at the hostel rooftop.

Varun is laughing a lot.

Eva: What is the funny story today?

Manoj: You better not say it.

Surender: I have heard but I am not sure. You must tell Varun.

Ekta: Yes, why do you guys have all the fun?

Varun: Ok, here you go. You know Manoj is used to reading alone. So last night, due to some electric fluctuations his tube light stopped working and today we had a quiz in the first class in the morning and he has left it to last minute preparations as we all do. Out of frustration, he thought of taking out one of the tube lights in the hostel row as there are a couple of tube lights there. But he ended up with an electric shock and that scared the hell out of him!

Eva: OMG, are you ok?

Varun: Yes, it was just a mild shock but the look he gave was so hilarious! We were smoking in the lobby a few steps away and rushed to see what happened but there was nothing serious.

Manoj: Why are you so silent today Nitish and what are you up to?

Nitish: Learning from your stories over the beer party, I developed a happiness vision and want to be happy forever.

Surender: That's an ambitious one! Good going.

Varun: Yes, but it is not going to be so easy. The Professors here are already trying to give us a lot of stress and first you need to take care of that.

Nitish: Yes, if I look at it from a professional success dimension, then I want to pass with good grades and get a good placement to start with.

Eva: Relax. There is not any economic or technology difficulty on campus for any of these goals you are talking about.

Ekta: But I think there are some student politics on these and social pressures on your time, so you need to keep an eye on time management.

Manoj: Yes, but there is not much of administrative issue and I don't see any legal troubles.

Surender: See, it's so easy to apply PEST in your case! Ha-ha.

External Environment Analysis

PEST Analysis

External Environment Analysis: The external environment is the macro environment in which an organization exists. One tool to analyse this environment is the PEST (political, economic, social and technological) analysis.

Application of PEST Analysis in the story: The PEST environment for students in campus is as follows.

Environmental Force	Impact on Nitish
Political	Yes there are tough politics.
Economic	It is almost similar for all.
Social	Yes there is peer pressure.
Technological	It's favorable for all.

Overall Impact: It is a tough environment.

It's your turn now: How is your PEST analysis for Happiness? How are you managing it? How you should manage it?

*****

A few days later.

In the human resource management class.

The Professor is taking attendance and someone makes a proxy for Varun.

Professor: *(In an irritated voice)* This is not done. You need to tell me who made this proxy for Varun.

And suddenly the class says Varun, Varun as Varun has just entered the class! Varun looks confused by so much attention on him.

And everyone bursts out in laughter. The Professor can't help but smile.

Same day, after dinner, while walking around in campus.

Nitish: I am not sure about getting good grades and good placements. What do you think?

Varun: Yes, the majority of our classmates are looking for the same. So it is going to be quite tough.

Eva: We all can do our best, but it's all in the hands of Professors when it comes to grades and that's beyond our control.

Ekta: Placements are in hands of recruiters. Big names are well established and beyond any influence for us.

Varun: On top of it, there are all these talks of artificial intelligence taking over our jobs and maybe getting a good placement might not be that easy!

Manoj: And on top of it, there are more executive MBA programs coming from IIMs, including new IIMs!

Surender: Wow! Here comes the industry analysis for you Nitish!

Industry Environment Analysis

Industry Environment Analysis: For industry analysis, the Five Force analysis tool is used. The collective strength of these five forces determines the ultimate profit potential or attractiveness of an industry.

Application in the story: Five force analysis for Nitish in the campus, taking his batch as the relevant industry, is as follows.

Force	Impact
Bargaining Power of Buyers	High
Bargaining Power of Suppliers	High
Rivalry	High
Threat of Substitute	Low but increasing
Threat of New Entrants	Moderate

Overall Impact: It is a highly competitive industry.

It's your turn now: What is your five force analysis for finding or maintaining Happiness? Is it favorable or unfavorable? How can you manage it better?

*****

Next day over lunch.

Eva: Nitish, I was thinking about your path to happiness. You should also introspect and find out what are your strengths and weaknesses.

Manoj: That makes sense. You are good in a number of things such as athletics and you have good health.

Ekta: And yes you are great in academics.

Varun: But you should also look at your weaknesses such as your short temper and shyness.

Surender: Yes, it is important to stay calm under pressure.

Ekta: And you should overcome your shyness too!

Nitish: Thank you guys for the heads up on me.

Internal Environment Analysis

Internal Environment Analysis: The self analysis of finding internal strengths and weaknesses of an organization is called internal environment analysis.

Application in the story: Nitish has some strengths such as good academics, analytical skills and good health. He has some shortcomings also such as a short temper and he is shy. This is an internal environment analysis.

It's your turn now: What are your strengths for finding or maintaining Happiness? What are your weaknesses for not finding or maintaining Happiness? How can you do better?

*****

In the evening, after dinner, while going around for a walk in campus;

Nitish: You won't believe what Varun did a few minutes ago!

Varun: Nothing happened. He is just exaggerating.

Ekta: There must be something for sure. Go ahead Nitish, spill the beans.

Nitish: Varun was trying to be friendly with the international students. And in a zeal to show how funny he is, he shared a joke on blondes in front of the international students and two of them are blondes. I tried to give him a hint but as you know when he is in the flow he doesn't listen. And you should have seen the confused looks on the face of the international students as to why on earth someone will be so rude!

Eva: That's so rude. But that serves you good Varun. You should mend your ways.

Varun: I didn't know they were blondes!

Ekat: Ha ha, way to go Varun! Someone definitely needs to teach him about that.

Surender: Ha ha, it happens sometime. Better be careful next time.

Varun: *(To shift the focus away from him)* Have you made any progress on your happiness strategy, Nitish?

Nitish: Yes, I am working on it.

Surender: I think you should not bother that much about your weaknesses. You need to see what you are good at and focus on that.

Eva: Yes, you have been good in studies, and are doing well in classes so far!

Ekta: And you are great in analytical abilities and have great communication skills, which would be good input in placements.

Manoj: Yes, you have good number of competencies and should focus on building these more.

Nitish: Thank you all, you are making it look so good for me.

Core Competence

Core Competence: Core Competencies of an organization are the collective learnings which differentiate one organization from another and are difficult to copy by others.

Application in the story: Nitish's core competencies are his learning ability, analytical skills and communication skills.

It's your turn now: What is your core competency for finding or maintaining Happiness? Where are you lacking? How are you making sure you nourish yourself and add more core competencies?

*****

Next day, in the finance class.

Rohit is a bit of a crazy student in the class.

A new young female guest Professor is discussing the basics of finance.

Rohit is a bit smitten by her beauty and is caught staring at her by the Professor.

Professor: (*Bit amused and confused and looking directly at Rohit*) Rohit, are you with us?

No reply by Rohit.

Professor: (*Bit irritated*) Are you listening to me? Can you summarize what I have discussed in last half an hour?

Rohit: (*Looks lost*) ...What is your question, please?

And the class laughs out loud.

Professor ignores him and the session continues.

Later, over dinner.

Varun: Nitish, let me play devil's advocate for your path to happiness. You cannot look only at your strengths; you need to look at your weaknesses too.

Nitish: Yes, I know I am not good at sales and would stay away from a sales job.

Ekta: Adding to the devil's advocate, don't mind it, honestly you need to work on your looks and grooming a bit, I mean your choice of formals.

Varun: You mean he doesn't have your flamboyant good taste? Just kidding, why don't you go and help him out the next time he goes shopping.

Eva: Yes, that's a good idea. Better you both help him out the next time he goes shopping.

Nitish: Yes, that would be a good help. Thank you.

Manoj: That completes your SWOT analysis!

SWOT Analysis

SWOT Analysis: Strength, Weakness, Opportunities and Threat or SWOT analysis looks in totality at both external as well as internal environment of an organization.

Application in the story: The SWOT analysis for Nitish is as follows.

Strengths	**Weaknesses**
Leaning abilities, Analytical abilities, Good academic record, Good health, Good communications	Short temper Shy No stand out personal style
Opportunities	**Threats**
Good campus placements Growing economy	Tough competition

It's your turn now: What is your SWOT analysis for finding or maintaining Happiness? How are you managing it? How you should do it?

*****

A few days later, over tea in the institute cafeteria.

The group is laughing about the marketing class.

In the marketing class, just a few minutes ago, the Professor started his presentation and asked a few questions from the students. Unknowingly, the presentation was moved to few sides ahead by the Professor about which he did not know. Those slides had the answers to those questions. When the Professor asked the questions from students, they answered by seeing it from the slides without making it very obvious. The Professor was looking in front and was very surprised that students are able to answer so easily.

Varun: I can't stop laughing over it. The Professor looked so impressed with our answers, though the answers were there on the slides right in front of us!

Ekta: Yes, it is hilarious.

Nitish: Yes, it was so funny. By the way I have done a good amount of analysis over the last weeks. I think, I need to work more on it.

Ekta: I think you need to find out how are you better than others in the class for your good grades and placements.

Varun: Yes, grades are relative as in comparison to others in class and for placements also you need to compete with the class and also in a way with students from other institutes.

Manoj: Take it easy. Do not over think. You are going to do well.

Competitive Advantage

Competitive Advantage: It refers to how one company is better than others in a given industry. Competitive advantage is creating a wider gap than your competition between the maximum price a buyer is willing to pay and the lowest price below which the supplier will not sell.

Application in the story: Nitish's core competencies put him in a better situation in the industry as he can add value using his learning abilities, analytical skills and focus. This is competitive advantage.

It's your turn now: What is your competitive advantage for finding or maintaining Happiness? How are you improving on it? How should you be doing it?

*****

In the classroom.

Ravi is this very young faculty who has joined only a few months ago. Students keep troubling him particularly by coming late and asking for attendance.

After waiting for five minutes he takes attendance and starts teaching.

After 15 minutes, Varun enters and requests for attendance too. The Professor looks irritated but marks him present and says I hope no one else will come after this.

Varun goes to the classroom door, closes it from inside and then says.

Varun: Now no one else will come!

The class breaks into a loud laughter.

The Professor looks irritated but continues with the class.

After the class, on the way to the hostel for lunch.

Eva: Nitish for your path to happiness, you should look at it not only from your perspective, but how your success is going to help the class or the corporate world. You should look at adding some value.

Surender: Bingo. I can't agree more.

Manoj: Yes, that does make sense.

Ekta: It's an interesting way to look at it!

Value Addition

Value Addition: Value addition means what value is added by an activity or an outside organization to an organization.

Application in the story: The value addition is through his learning abilities, analytical skills and focused approach.

It's your turn now: What is your value addition to your Happiness? How are you improving on it? How should you be doing it?

*****

A few days later over drinks on a Friday evening in Cyber Hub.

While they are waiting for the snacks, Varun gets a phone call from an unknown number and his phone shows the caller as a spammer and bank scammer.

Caller: This is a phone call from *** bank and it is regarding your ATM card.

Varun: (*Knowing full well that it is a scam call, puts the call on speaker, in a very submissive and frightened voice*) Yes ... Yes, sir, is there something wrong?

Caller: (*In an authoritative voice*) Yes, the information for the card is not correct and we are going to cancel your card unless you reconfirm your information.

Varun: Sir, I am a poor illiterate man (*Winks at Nitish*). I might have done it by mistake. Please tell me what information you need.

Caller: Ok, tell me your card number, the name on it, and its CVV code.

Varun: Sir, please hold the phone for 4-5 minutes and I will give you the information. I need to find the card first.

Caller: You call me after 5 minutes.

Varun: Sir, my phone doesn't have any balance left for making calls. Please don't cut the call. I will find it in 2-3 minutes. Please.

Caller: (*a bit irritated*) Ok, do it quickly.

Varun puts the phone aside and the whole group smiles.

Ekta: (*In a whispering voice*) Yes this is the way to teach them a lesson.

The group gets their snacks. After five minutes.

Varun: I am so sorry sir, please give me two more minutes.

Caller: (*A bit irritated*) Ok, do it quickly.

Varun puts the phone aside and the whole group smiles and continues with the snacks and beer.

After 3 minutes.

Varun: Looks like it is in the wallet of my father. He has gone for a walk. He will be back in 2 minutes. Please hold for 2 more minutes.

Caller: (*very irritated*) You are so irresponsible. I am a busy bank officer and I don't have any more time for you.

Varun: (In *a pleading voice*) Please sir, give me 2 more minutes, please. I have only this card and I will be in trouble if you cancel it.

Caller: (*Irritated*) Ok, do it quickly.

Varun puts the phone aside and the whole group smiles.

After 3 minutes.

Varun: (*In a very apologetic voice*) Sir, please forgive me for keeping you on wait. My father is back but the card is not with him. The card is with my wife who has gone to work in a neighbour's house and she will be back in 2 minutes. Please give me a last chance. Please.

Caller: (*In a very rude and irritated voice*) You are so disorganised. You cannot find a card in last 20 minutes. I don't have any more time.

Varun: (*In a pleading voice*) Sir, you are like a big brother to me. You look a very well educated and large hearted person. Please help me by giving me 2 more minutes. I have sent my son to get the card from my wife. Please, give me 2 more minutes.

Caller: (*In a very boastful voice*) Ok, do it fast.

Varun: (*In an apologetic voice*) Yes sir, just a few minutes.

And Varun puts the phone away.

The group laughs out loud.

Varun: I must have wasted 25 or more minutes of his time and saved some gullible people from him.

After few more drinks.

Nitish: It is all so frustrating at times. I am not making as much progress as I was planning.

Varun: Yes, that must be frustrating.

Eva: Relax. Have you tried to find the reasons behind it?

Nitish: Yes, I tried. Maybe I am not managing my resources, particularly time so well.

Ekta: Then Surender is the best one to tell you about discipline of time management!

Surender: Chill! Keep it simple. See all the things you want to do, and resources available and allot them in accordance of importance and urgency. Enjoy the drinks for now.

Manoj: Yes, keep it simple man. Cheers!

Value Chain Analysis

Value Chain Analysis: Value chain analysis is a detailed analysis of each activity of an organization on the criteria of the cost of the activity and value created by the activity, and reconfiguring the activities in a way that it creates competitive advantage for the organization.

Application in the story: The value chain of the story from his perspective is given below.

<table>
<tr><td rowspan="4">Secondary Activities</td><td colspan="5">Technology
Network connection, wi-fi, mobile apps, laptops.</td></tr>
<tr><td colspan="5">Human Resource Management
His network</td></tr>
<tr><td colspan="5">Procurement
Reading material</td></tr>
<tr><td colspan="5">Firm Infrastructure
Good health, analytical skills, learning abilities, focus.</td></tr>
<tr><td>Primary Activities</td><td>Inbound Logistics</td><td>Operations</td><td>Outbound Logistics</td><td>Marketing & Sales</td><td>Service</td></tr>
<tr><td></td><td>Gathering reading material & information</td><td>Studying, Networking</td><td>Good grades & placement chances</td><td>Continuously reinforcing his credentials in academics</td><td>Investing in maintaining the network</td></tr>
</table>

It's your turn now: What is your value chain for your new or existing Happiness? What are the activities you need to remove? What are the activities you should focus on?

* * * * *

It is Sunday morning and the group goes for the Delhi half marathon run on India Gate. They all run for three kilometers. After running they sit down for breakfast in Lodhi Restaurant, a nice restaurant on Lodhi Road which is few kilometers from India Gate.

Varun: So what's up with you Nitish. Are you still busy with your analysis?

Nitish: I have done lot of analysis over the last few weeks. Now I need a break!

Eva: Yes, I bet you need one. Enjoy your breakfast for now.

Manoj: Sure. But you are so young, maybe you can try your hands at a startup and Varun can give you some insights.

Varun: Oh man, don't go there!

Ekta: Ok then, just pass me some sausage.

Strategic Alternatives and Choice

Strategic Alternatives and Choice: Strategic alternatives means an organization creates and evaluates various strategic options to achieve its stated vision and mission. And later chooses one strategy out of these alternatives.

Application in the story: Nitish has various alternatives. One is to focus on good grades and getting a good placement. Another one is to go for his own startup. He chooses to go with good grades and a good placement.

It's your turn now: Which part of life you are currently focused on for Happiness? What are your alternatives? Which one you should focus on?

*****

Later that afternoon, over beer and lunch in Hauskhas village, a party place on the way back to the Institute.

Eva: Nitish for your path to happiness, are you not focusing too much on material stuff. It looks all good in the beginning but this mad rat race kills you in number of ways. I have seen it myself.

Manoj: Yes, you need to balance out.

Surender: I can't agree more. Also try looking for a girl too for yourself.

Ekta: You stay out of it, if you are looking for a happy life! It's all so overhyped!

Varun: There are happy couples too!

Manoj: Yes, go for it Nitish!

Strategy Levels

Strategy Levels: Strategy operates at three levels namely, corporate level i.e. overall organization and its business units, business level i.e. at level of a business unit and functional level i.e. for various functional areas of a business unit such as marketing, finance, operations and human resources.

Application in the story: Nitish needs to choose at three levels i.e. for overall happiness i.e. 5 D happiness and that is his corporate strategy. There are four types of corporate strategies. He chooses to focus on professional success, which is a growth strategy for him as he is looking to make it big.

Once he has decided to go for professional success, then he needs to choose among multiple options, among differentiation, low cost and niche strategy. He is focusing on differentiation. This is business strategy.

After that he needs to decide about how to manage time and expenses (finance), friends (human resource), classes, assignments, grades, placements (operations), and his image (marketing) for the good grades and placements. These are his functional strategies.

It's your turn now: What is your overall strategy for Happiness? What is your strategy for professional success happiness? What is your strategy for managing time and finances, your friends, managing meetings, image etc. for Happiness?

*****

A few days later.

Varun gets this very funny ring tone of a crying little girl on his mobile phone. And he generally keeps his volume high.

Varun volunteers to show the campus to a group of five foreign dignitaries. They reach the library.

Varun: Before we enter the library, please put your phones on silent mode. We students take the library very seriously and spend a lot of time here and it's our unwritten ritual to maintain complete silence in the library, and particularly in the reading room where everyone is studying.

The visitors nod their head in agreement and they also look impressed with Varun.

They enter the library reading hall and at the very moment, there is a loud sound of a crying baby as Varun's phone rings! There is a loud laughter in the reading room. The dignitaries first look a bit confused but then laugh out loud. Varun sheepishly switch offs his phone.

Later over coffee at the institute cafeteria, the group is laughing over this funny incident.

Ekta: Varun you are impossible.

Eva: It happens, just chill.

Varun: (*To change focus from him*) What's going with you Nitish? Have you made any progress on your analysis?

Nitish: I am done with a part of it. I chose to focus on good grades, developing my case solving and analytical abilities further and harness my learning skills to differentiate myself for strategy roles either in consulting firms or on the corporate side.

Manoj: Yes, you are putting a lot of time and energy efforts on this.

Surender: I am sure you will make it after all this hard work.

Differentiation Strategy

Differentiation Strategy: When your scope is wider and you are competing on creating something different or unique from others, it is differentiation strategy. In this, the organization spends resources to produce goods of unique features valued by customers who are willing to pay a higher price for that.

Application in the story: Nitish is investing a lot of time and efforts to be unique and different in ways that Professors and recruiters appreciate. He is following a differentiation strategy.

It's your turn now: Are you following a differentiation strategy for Happiness? What is your differentiation strategy? What should it be?

*****

A few days later, over an evening walk in the campus.

The group is still laughing about the afternoons event.

The rehearsal for the Institute annual fest is going on and Rohit, the crazy student, is doing this mono-acting which is quite boring and the students are just waiting for it to finish.

Suddenly, Varun with some other classmates form a small human chain and it enters from the last of the sitting rows and stops in the front, break into dances and claps for some time which sees the end of the boring mono-acting of Rohit.

The audience laughs out loud.

After walking for some more time.

Eva: Focusing too much on professional success is not my cup of tea.

Manoj: I have learned the hard way to take it easy. My priority is to put minimum efforts in time and energy and be happy with whatever I get.

Ekta: Yes, that makes sense. We are not here to just work and work.

Surender: Well I can't agree more. Life is much bigger than just professional success.

Cost Leadership Strategy

Cost Leadership Strategy: To sustain against rivals in the industry, the concept of competitive strategy is used. There are two variables namely competitive scope and competitive advantage. There are three generic possibilities of Low cost leadership, differentiation and focus. When your scope is wider and you are competing on low cost is called cost leadership strategy. In this, the organization produces goods or services of comparable features at low cost compared to the competition in the industry.

Application in the story: Manoj is following a cost leadership strategy. He is spending less resources on getting good placements and is happy with whatever he gets. Based on his track record, he will get a reasonable job, without putting as many resources as others are putting.

It's your turn now: Are you following a cost leadership strategy for Happiness? What is your cost leadership strategy? What should it be?

* * * * *

A few days later.

It is the opening ceremony of the 2-day annual festival of the Institute. It is time to start with welcoming the guests and Varun takes the mike.

Varun: (*At full speed*) It is my immense pleasure to invite you to the closing ceremony of the event and propose my vote of thanks!

Audience roars in laughter.

Varun realizes he has taken the wrong piece of paper by mistake. He welcomes the audience.

After dinner on the same day. They are laughing about the morning incident.

Ekta: Ha ha, Varun that was a very funny welcome!

Manoj: Sure it was.

Varun: (*to change focus from him)*, What are you going to do after MBA?

Eva: Yes, tell us. You seem to have a plan.

Surender: I am thinking of working for some religious organization.

Manoj: That's an interesting perspective.

Ekta: At least you will get some peace of mind there!

Niche Strategy

Niche or Focus Strategy: When your scope is narrow, it is called niche strategy.

Application in the story: There are few religious organizations as compared to number of business organizations and these religious organizations are not run by management graduates. Surender wants to join only one of the religious organisation. He is following a niche strategy.

It's your turn now: Are you following a niche strategy for Happiness? What is your niche strategy? What should it be?

*****

Recently, a new stray dog (it is named Buddy by the students) entered the campus and keeps hanging out everywhere. It has literally attended all kind of activities going from a regular lecture to a student activity.

There is a guest session for the batch by the CEO of a MNC.

In the auditorium.

Nitish: I hope we have made all the arrangements that the dog doesn't enter the auditorium today as the guest speaker might not like it.

Varun: Yes, today it won't be able to attend. The organizers have made a lot of efforts to keep him out– closed the doors, scared him with sticks, got the security monitoring him etc.

Ekta: That's sad.

Varun: He is almost everywhere. And he spends more time in the Library than I do! I think it should be also given a degree this year!

All laugh about it.

And then the guest enters the auditorium with the dog! And the class laughs out loud.

The dog had just appeared on the red carpet in front of the guest and the guest happened to be a dog lover and he brought the dog inside the auditorium with him.

After the guest session, over lunch, in the institute canteen.

Ekta: The compulsory guest session by placements was a complete waste of time today. The life here is going crazy with so many assignments and compulsory guest sessions!

Manoj: I think management schools are over doing it. There is no need for so many courses, and so many assignments in each course and compulsory guest sessions. It's almost impossible to do justice to all of these in the limited time we have.

Eva: Looks like management schools have lost on strategy!

Nitish: Yes, that is what it looks like! At least I have a strategy for myself, finally!

Surender: That's great going.

Varun: Wow, nice.

Eva: That's good news. I am happy for you.

Strategy

Strategy: Strategy is choosing a unique position among various alternatives possible and staying focused on that to achieve the desired vision.

Application in the story: Nitish vision is to be a successful professional and for that he invests in building his abilities, skills and knowledge as well as good grades to get a good placement. This is strategy.

It's your turn now: Do you have a strategy for finding or maintaining Happiness? What is your strategy for Happiness? What should it be?

*****

Next day, in the class room.

It is in the middle of a session. Varun enters the class, in slippers, t-shirt and half pants, which is made out by cutting his jean. He is followed by Nitish.

The class laughs out loud.

Professor looks confused by the turn of events.

Professor: What happened, don't you know the dress code and that half pants are not allowed.

Varun: I know sir, but I fell over the stairs today morning and my left knee got bruised and doctor has advised to keep it open for speedy recovery.

Professor: Oh, in that case, take your seat. Mowgli! *(The character from Jungle book)*

The class laughs out loud.

And the session continues.

After the session, over lunch.

Varun: Where is Nitish, he is not taking lunch today?

Eva: He was in hurry and left without lunch to meet a consultant in Mckinsey.

Surender: Yes, he was telling he has made some mentors from industry in the last few months.

Ekta: Yes, he was getting a lot of industry insights from them.

Manoj: That's a smart move.

Tactics

Tactics: Tactics are short terms activities for supporting and achieving the chosen strategy of an organization.

Application in the story: It is very important to understand how the industry works and for that Nitish has got some mentors from industry. This is called tactics as it is a step towards achieving his strategy of being a successful professional.

It's your turn now: What are your tactics for Happiness? Do these help in Happiness strategy? What should be your tactics?

*****

In a nearby Starbucks Cafe, on Thursday afternoon.

Nitish: I am trying to stay focused on the professional success front but even doing that looks so complex.

Eva: Yes, nothing worthwhile comes easy. What is the problem you are facing now?

Manoj: He is trying to manage resources of time, and energy among various options available for professional success.

Varun: Yes, he is too much into live projects with industry and good grades.

Ekta: Good grades and live projects are his forte and they are valued by industry and recruiters.

Surender: Maybe you can use your past reputation and grades to build more industry networking where you are not that good.

Eva: Yes, you can spend minimum time and energy on useless theoretical cut and paste group projects.

Nitish: Oh, you have done BCG analysis for me! Great and thanks.

BCG Matrix

BCG Matrix: It is a tool used in corporate strategy for portfolio planning of business units of an organisation. It is based on the market growth rates and relative market shares and classifies the business units into four categories i.e. star, cash cow, dog and question mark.

Application in the story: Treating time and efforts as the main resource.

BCG matrix for Nitish is given below.

High	**Stars** Good grades Live projects	**Cash Cows** Past reputation and grades
Market Share Low	**Question Marks** (?) Industry networking	**Dogs** Just theoretical cut and paste Group projects.
	High	Low
	Market Growth Rate	

It's your turn now: Do you have a BCG matrix for Happiness? What is it? What should it be?

*****

It is Friday evening and the group has gone to watch a movie. While driving back to the institute.

Nitish: I am very impressed by the guest speaker today. I never thought innovation is that important and it can be learned.

Eva: Yes, that's right. What are you going to do about it?

Nitish: I think I need to widen my options. I am going to build on my skills for innovation and that would open up more opportunities for me.

Manoj: Take it easy. You are already working quite hard.

Surender: I agree with Nitish. You are quite young and you should take innovation seriously if you intend to stay for long in the corporate sector.

Ekta: Yes, I agree. You should diversify your options in the language of your strategy Professor Husmukh.

Varun: Yes, I think you should use Ansoff matrix to diversify.

Eva: Yes, that's the way. Now we need to complete the remaining part of the case presentation for tomorrow.

Diversification (Ansoff Matrix)

Ansoff Matrix: It gives the various ways in which a company can expand its business. For existing markets or new markets and existing products or new products, it creates four possibilities of market penetration, market expansion, product expansion and diversification. Diversification is one way of growth for an organization when it goes into newer businesses which may or may not relate to its current business.

Application in the story: The Ansoff Matrix for Nitish is given below.

Markets		
New	Look for outside campus placements too.	Look for some international placements outside campus placements.
Existing	Intelligence, analysis, hard work, good grades.	Innovation skills and ability to innovate.
	Existing	New
	Products	

It's your turn now: Do you have an Ansoff matrix for Happiness? What is it? What should it be?

*****

Next day. It is strategy class and the group of six are making a presentation on Strategy for India.

Eva and Manoj have run through half of the presentation. Varun looks bored and is looking sleepy.

Professor Doordarshi: Now Varun you tell us the key take away so far from the presentation.

Varun is caught by surprise and looks completely lost. And the class bursts in a loud laughter.

Varun: They were talking about China.

And the class again bursts in a loud laughter.

Professor: Seriously, you mean it?

Varun: Yes, sir, this is what they are discussing. How China and India are neighbors and their strategy.

And the class again bursts in a loud laughter.

Professor: Are they not talking about Strategy in India.

Varun: Yes, that's what I am saying. Strategy in India for China and strategy in China for India.

And the class again bursts in a loud laughter.

The Professor asks him to take presentations more seriously otherwise he will be in trouble. And Varun agrees with him.

After the class, over coffee in the Institute canteen.

Ekta: How many times have I told you to show some interest in the group presentations. You are a complete free rider in our group.

Eva: Yes, Varun you need to take it more seriously.

Varun: Yes, next time I will try. (*And to change the focus from him*) Going back to our discussion last night, Nitish how are you actually going to develop your innovation ability?

Eva: There must be some way.

Nitish: I have thought about it and I am going to do an internship with our innovation Professor Doordarshi for his book on innovators and his consultancy assignments on innovations so that I will get a feel of both theory and practice.

Manoj: Yes, that's a good strategic alliance you are thinking of.

Ekta: That looks good to me. Carry on.

Strategic Alliances

Strategic Alliances: It is the coming together of two or more organizations for mutual gain. When these two organizations form a separate legal entity then that kind of alliance is called a joint venture.

Application in the story: Professor Doordarshi needs some assistance for his work on the book on innovators and in consultancy assignments on innovation and Nitish needs to learn and this is an example of strategic alliance.

It's your turn now: Do you have a strategic alliance for Happiness? What is it? What should it be?

*****

One week later, over lunch in the Institute canteen.

Ekta and Eva can't stop laughing.

Varun: What are you hiding from us?

Ekta: It is not about you. We are laughing about the situation in our hostel for last three days. The Girl hostel warden's mother has got dengue and the warden for the boy's hostel is given additional charge for few days. It turns out to be quite funny as each time the warden visits the hostel, an announcement is made by the old female peon in the hostel corridors that the warden sir is going to be here soon! She does it so diligently and seriously that it looks as if some Mughal Emperor is going to come.

The group laughs out loud.

Eva: Yes, the poor soul tries her best to make sure that girls know that the warden is going to be inside the hostel and accordingly girls need to behave! But her way is so hilarious!

Nitish: Yes, it is so funny.

Varun: By the way, I ended up attending the marriage of one of my friends last week. He is a successful startup owner and he married another startup owner.

Eva: Well, that's cool.

Varun: My guess is he is going to combine the two startups.

Ekta: I would never mix the two. If you can handle one at a time, it is more than enough.

Manoj: Well I agree with you. Ideally it looks good on paper, but in practice it might create more problems for the two.

Nitish: Mixing business and personal life might not be a great idea.

Varun: I think they are smart and are planning to merge the two organizations and come up with a third one to give equal space to each other.

Ekta: Oh Ok. Let's see how it goes.

Mergers and Acquisitions

Mergers and Acquisitions: It is one of the ways for an organization to grow. If an organization takes over some another organization, then it is called an acquisition and if two organizations become a third new organization then it is called a merger.

Application in the story: As discussed in the story above, it looks like a case of merger as both want to create a third organization by merging the two separate organizations.

It's your turn now: Do you have any acquisition for Happiness? What is it? What should it be?

*****

Same day, later in the evening, on the badminton court.

Ekta: It was surprising to see Nitish with his main rival Rohit last night. What were you up to?

Varun: He is a smart chap. He needs to go to meet his industry mentor next Monday and Professor Ravi has scheduled a quiz on that day. And his main rival also needs to go home to attend some family function. Am I right Nitish?

Nitish: Yes, we were exploring options to get the quiz postponed.

Eva: Wow, what a good example of co-opetition!

Surender: It is a good move.

Co-opetition

Co-opetition: Co-opetition is the strategy of competing as well as co-operating with your competition on certain things for mutual gains.

Application in the story: Nitish and his main rival Rohit are mostly competing. However, he need to go to meet his industry mentor next Monday and Professor Ravi has scheduled a quiz on that day. And Rohit also needs to go home to attend some family function. And they come together to have cooperation to solve this problem. This is co-opetition.

It's your turn now: Do you have a Co-opetition strategy for Happiness? What is it? What should it be?

*****

A few days later, it is time for mid-term exams. The group focuses on studying for the exams.

A day before the examination on sales, a school friend of Varun comes to meet him and they end up going for a drink. The plan was to have only one drink and catch up. But they ended up drinking till late evening and getting drunk.

Next day in the exam, Varun goes without any preparation. And used his friends' advice that come whatever question keep going around with stories using certain words again and again such as customer focus, customer experience and involvement, delighting the customer, understanding the customer and taking customer feedback; and fill sufficient number of pages. And that's all you need.

And somehow it worked too for him!

A day after mid-term exams. After dinner, during a walk in the campus.

Varun: Hey guys, I am not sure about how this placement thing is going to come out in the end.

Manoj: You are unnecessarily worried. It is going to be ok.

Nitish: I agree with Varun. It is not going to be that simple to get the kind of placement that I am looking for.

Eva: Then what are you going to do about it.

Nitish: Well, I am learning innovation skills and will figure out something. Maybe I can create a Blue Ocean strategy for me.

Ekta: Great thought. But that's not easy.

Nitish: Yes, but I am working on it.

Varun: Maybe I can learn some tricks from you.

Ekta: Sure, there is always scope for improvement.

Nitish: I am happy to share as we all are friends.

Blue Ocean Strategy

Blue Ocean Strategy: Blue Ocean strategy is to make competition irrelevant through innovations. It involves identifying the factors on which the industry is competing and then eliminating, reducing or raising these factors; and creating new factors, based on customer requirements.

Application in the story: The Blue Ocean creation for Nitish is given below. The students are competing on various factors for getting placements such as business school brand, grades, subject knowledge, live projects, analytical abilities, application orientation, industry knowledge etc. Nitish blue ocean strategy is given here.

Blue Ocean Component	**Action**
Eliminate	Not Applicable
Reduce	Too much focus on Analysis and Grades.
Raise	Industry knowledge and application of subject knowledge.
Create	Intuition, innovation abilities.

It's your turn now: Do you have a Blue Ocean strategy for Happiness? What is it? What should it be?

*****

A few days later, on a Friday afternoon, over tea in the Institute canteen.

Varun: Nitish, how is your analysis for the path to happiness going?

Nitish: It is so-so.

Varun: Oh. What is your business model to crack the recruitment process for final placements?

Nitish: Well, my value proposition is my innovation ability to solve complex problems. I need to figure out the rest.

Eva: That's a good start. Let us give you our inputs. Your delivery channel are emails, phone calls and personal visits.

Manoj: Great. You need to build customer relationships by continuous interactions.

Ekta: Your key activities involve building on your innovation skills, learning how things work, build an impressive CV and reach out to target customer group.

Surender: Your key resources are your skill set, good academic records, and friends like us.

Nitish: And my key partners are industry mentors, Professors, and placement agencies.

Varun: Your costs are time, energy and money spent on doing all these things and revenue is the expected salary and satisfaction.

Eva: See it is easy!

Nitish: Yes, you all make it look so easy. Thanks a lot. Cheers!!!

Business Model

Business Model: A business model is the way an organization identifies target customers, creates value for them and makes some profit out of this. A detailed concept is a business model canvas which consists of nine blocks.

Application in the story: The business model for Nitish is given below.

<table>
<tr>
<td rowspan="2">Key Partners

Industry Mentors, Professor Husmukh Doordarshis, Placement agencies</td>
<td>Key Activities

Innovation skills building. Learning how things work.</td>
<td rowspan="2">Value Proposition

Innovation ability to solve complex problems.</td>
<td>Customer Relationship

Management Relationship development by continuous interactions.</td>
<td rowspan="2">Customer Segment

Recruiters</td>
</tr>
<tr>
<td>Key Resources

Skill set, Friends, Education records.</td>
<td>Delivery

Emails, Phone, personal visits.</td>
</tr>
<tr>
<td colspan="3">Cost

Time, Energy, Efforts, Money.</td>
<td colspan="2">Revenue

Expected salary/job, satisfaction.</td>
</tr>
</table>

It's your turn now: Do you have a business model for Happiness? What is it? What should it be?

*****

In the night, in the hostel room, Nitish is reflecting.

It is two months now in this place. I think I am making the right moves and going in the right direction. Yes, it looks so. I have completed my strategy for happiness and it feels so good to finish it. Tomorrow I will go and share it with strategy Professor Doordarshi for his feedback…Also, I have made couple of good friends... This MBA is turning out to be more fun than I had imagined.

His mind keeps going over all kind of thoughts till he falls asleep.

*****

Happiness Masterclass 5

Happiness is a choice, make happiness a habit and create happiness tools to stay happy

It's all in the mind and body too. It is within you. And it can be harnessed, developed and created through regular practice.

There are different tools. Identify what works for you from; meditation, yoga, sports, spending time with friends and family, occasional drinks, travel, and, even inspirational readings. You need to smile more and show your gratitude for what you have.

Part V

Correct Path To Happiness

(Realigning Strategy Formulation)

In the office of Professor Husmukh Doordarshi.

Nitish: Good evening Professor Doordarshi. Thanks for your time. I have worked on happiness and I think my happiness strategy is ready.

Professor Doordarshi: Great! That's nice to hear. So what is your happiness strategy?

Nitish: As suggested by you, I have written it down and here it is for you.

Professor Doordarshi takes the document and goes through it quickly.

Professor Doordarshi: Well, it is a good beginning.

Nitish: Oh, you really think so?

Professor Doordarshi: Well, there is a mistake you have made which most of us make. You are talking of happiness but so far you have looked only at one part of happiness. You remember your definition of happiness?

Nitish: Yes, it has five dimensions. Oh, I got it. I focused only on one part i.e. career. It is a blunder.

Professor Doordarshi: It is OK. Most of us make the same mistake. Good thing is you have realized your mistake. Go and work upon it.

Nitish: Yes, I am going to work on it.

Professor Doordarshi: You have already worked on your professional success part. Now focus on the rest of the four dimensions.

Nitish: Yes, I am going to start with health next.

Professor Doordarshi: Wait a minute. Here is some great research material for a good health. You first read these and look for some more seminal work, discuss among your friends and come back.

*****

Health

Nitish reads all the material suggested by Professor Doordarshi and discusses it with his friends and also watches some TED talks and analyses all these inputs.

A week later in the office of Professor Doordarshi.

Nitish: Good afternoon, Professor. I have worked on the health dimension and here is my outcome.

There are five parts to my health strategy for happiness.

- Mind Matters: It's all in the mind and so some kind of meditation for 10 minutes to start with, and a positive attitude is my plan.
- Fitness: A fit body needs exercises that focus on stamina (running, jogging, cycling, swimming etc.), strength (gym) and flexibility (Yoga, badminton etc.). 5 hours a week is my plan.
- Diet: As suggested by a good dietician.
- Sleep: Minimum 6 hours of sleep.

- Disease Free: A regular annual checkup.

Professor Doordarshi: It looks good so far.

Now take this material I have for you on relationships, and ponder over it.

Nitish: Thanks a lot.

*****

Relationships

Nitish reads all the material suggested by Professor Doordarshi. He watches interesting TED talks and YouTube videos. Discusses it with his friends and analyses all these inputs.

A week later in the office of Professor Doordarshi.

Nitish: Good afternoon, Professor. I have worked on the relationship dimension and here is my outcome.

There are five parts to my relationship strategy for happiness.

- Priority Setting: These relationships are my priority and I am going to keep reminding myself about this on a daily basis.
- Gratitude: Need to show gratitude and say thanks more often to friends and family for being there.
- Regular investment: I am going to make it a point to invest regularly in relationships and giving some gifts.
- Staying in touch: I am going to spend some time on the telephone on a daily basis say 15 minutes with my family and 15 minutes with my three best friends. I am going to meet my family and my three

best friends at least once in every three months or maybe more.

- Doing things together: I am going to do some activities with them such as movies, travel, eating out etc. Whatever, the situation, if my best friends or family is in town, then my Saturday is booked only for them.

Professor Doordarshi: Good going.

Here is some interesting material for you on spirituality/religion.

Nitish: Thanks a lot Professor.

*****

Spirituality/Religion

Nitish starts with watching TED talks, and some funny YouTube videos. Then he reads all the materials suggested by Professor Husmukh. After that he takes interesting inputs from Surender and analyses all these inputs.

A week later in the office of Professor Husmukh Doordarshi.

Nitish: Good afternoon, Professor. I have worked on the spirituality/ religion dimension and here is my outcome.

There are three parts to my spirituality/religion strategy for happiness.

- Gratitude: I believe in god but not rituals. So I am going to give 5 minutes every day to show gratitude to god for all his blessings.
- Friendship: I look at it as a friendship with God and not as a begging relationship.

- Developing a Portfolio: I am going to read more on this topic, and get more exposure to it in the future and then develop a portfolio of activities around spirituality/ religion.

This is not my priority area as of now. I am just making a beginning and commitment to this.

Professor Doordarshi: It is a good beginning. You are moving in the right direction. Here is some interesting material for you on Philanthropy.

*****

Philanthropy

Nitish starts his discussions with Eva and gets a lot of good material too from Eva. He also reads the material suggested by Professor Husmukh and analyses all these inputs.

A week later in the office of Professor Doordarshi.

Nitish: Good afternoon, Professor. I have worked on the philanthropy dimension and here is my outcome.

There are three parts to my philanthropy strategy for happiness.

- Starting a Money Donation Habit: It is all about starting a habit. I am starting with 100 rupees a week.
- Starting a Time Donation Habit: I am starting with 1 hour of time per week.
- Building a Portfolio: I intend to develop a portfolio of philanthropy as my age and resources increase.

This is not my priority area as of now. I am just making a beginning and commitment to this.

Professor Doordarshi: It is a good beginning.

Nitish: Thanks a lot Professor. You are a great help.

*****

Nitish: These are the five dimensions of my happiness. Right now, my top priority areas are work, health and relationships. My low priority areas are philanthropy and religion/spirituality. In terms of corporate strategy, my high growth strategy is for work and health, stability strategy is for relationships and a low growth strategy is for philanthropy and religion/spirituality as I have not worked on these two yet. I am not planning any retrenchment strategy. In terms of my business strategy I am going to make efforts and spend resources on professional success, health and relationships as these are my differentiated strategy and would spend a bit of resources on religion/spirituality and philanthropy as I am following a low cost strategy for now.

Professor Doordarshi: Well, it is a good start. Now you need to implement it.

*****

The Five Principles

Next day, in the office of Professor Doordarshi.

Professor Doordarshi: You have made a lot of progress. Now you need to put it all together for having your five dimensional happiness.

Nitish: Well, you have been a great help. But I am not sure how to put all these things together.

Professor Doordarshi: Don't worry. It is normal to have this confusion. To put all these together, you need to follow five principles.

Nitish: Great! What are these five principles? I am very curious to know.

Principle # 1. Be aware and stay focused

Professor Doordarshi: Here we go. First principle

1. Be aware and stay focused.

Nitish: What do you mean?

Professor Doordarshi: The starting point is to know what you want and be aware of it and then stay focused on achieving it.

Nitish: Yes, it makes sense.

Nitish: Please share the second principle.

Principle # 2. Resource allocation and management.

Professor Doordarshi: Here we go. Second principle

2. Resource Allocation and Management.

We all have limited resources and you need to give sufficient resources to all the five dimensions of happiness.

Mostly we make the mistake of giving all or the majority of resources to only one or two dimensions.

Nitish: Yes, I agree. But it looks difficult as I am finding it so tough to find sufficient resources for even only one dimension of happiness.

Professor Doordarshi: You need to think through it. I suggest, you list down all your daily activities and resource spent on them for a week. Then you remove those activities which are not adding anything to any of the five dimensions of happiness. You need to be very prudent with your resources, particularly time.

Nitish: That's a great idea! I am on it now. I am going to list down all my activities and resources spent over the next one week and remove those activities which are not adding anything to any of the five dimensions of happiness.

Nitish: What is the third principle, Professor?

Principle # 3. You need to check regularly your progress and stay open to make changes.

Professor Doordarshi: Here we go. Third principle

3. You need to check regularly your progress and stay open to make changes.

Nitish: What do you mean?

Professor Doordarshi: For example, have a 1-minute happiness test three times a day, in the morning, after lunch and before going to bed. In that focus on your breath and ask yourself only one thing: Are you happy? And if you are not, then focus on working on it. Same with your strategy, as you need to keep track of the changing environment and accordingly check your assumptions and strategy.

Nitish: I got your point. And I can do a detailed analysis on a weekly and monthly basis.

Professor Doordarshi: Yes, there you go.

Nitish: Please share the fourth principle.

Principle # 4. Embrace Failures and Setbacks.

Professor Doordarshi: Here you go. Fourth principle.

4. Embrace Failures and Setbacks.

Nitish: I don't get it.

Professor Doordarshi: You need to take life easy and understand that success and failures are part of life. You should be open and ready for failures and disappointments, and accept it as part of the learning process. Eventually you will win, if you stay focused on your efforts without getting distracted or disheartened by failures and setbacks. Same with strategy.

Nitish: Please share the fifth principle.

Principle # 5. Keep it simple.

Professor Doordarshi: Here we go. Fifth principle

5. Keep it simple.

Professor Doordarshi: Don't over complicate strategy and life. Even if you don't want it to, life makes itself complicated. So from your side, you don't mess it further. Same with strategy. Same with happiness.

Nitish: Yes, I got your point.

*****

Later in the afternoon, in the library.

Nitish is synthesizing on what he has learned so far on his path to happiness.

After lot of reflections, and synthesis, he comes out with his strategy document for the path to happiness.

Strategy Document for the Path to Happiness

Vision To be and stay a happy person.				
Mission While being happy, to contribute in whatsoever small way to the happiness of the world.				
Core Values Respect, love and care for fellow human beings and the larger universe.				
Corporate Level Strategy: Growth				
Work	**Health**	**Relationships**	**Religion/ Spirituality**	**Philan-thropy**
High Growth Strategy	Medium Growth Strategy	Low to medium Growth Strategy	Low Growth Strategy	Very Low Growth Strategy
Business Level Strategy				
Work	**Health**	**Relationships**	**Religion/ Spirituality**	**Philan-thropy**
Differenti-ation	Differen-tiation	Differentiation	Niche low cost	Niche low cost

*****

Happiness Masterclass 6

Embrace Failures and Setbacks.

Always remember nothing is permanent and one is not a failure till one fails within. Stay passionate about your work and efforts but keep a sense of detachment from results.

Tomorrow is another day full of newer opportunities. Celebrate your failures for teaching you valuable insights. Create tools to get over failures fast such as the let it go formula (e.g. 3 deep breaths) to tackle any onset of stress on you.

Part VI

The Obstacles To Happiness

(Strategy Execution)

A few days later, in the evening over tea in the Institute canteen.

Nitsh: I have something to share. As all of you know, I was working on my happiness stuff. I have completed it!

Eva: Great! I am so proud of you.

Varun: Implementation is where all the fun begins. So watch your moves now onwards very carefully.

Ekta: Don't worry. A good beginning is half the work done. You have found the path to happiness and that's great!

Surender: Yes, do follow it and I am sure you will get good results.

Manoj: Yes, it is a good thing that you are doing. Wish I could have done it in my Institute days.

Nitish: I am also creating a daily routine for myself which will accumulate in a weekly routine which will further accumulate in a monthly routine and so forth. I am calling it a happy day commitment chart.

Strategy Execution

Strategy Execution: It is the process of implementing the chosen strategy, to reach the desired vision. Strategy execution is where the real fun in strategy beings.

Application in the story: Nitish is ready with his happiness strategy and now going to implement it. This is called strategy execution.

It's your turn now: Do you have an execution strategy for Happiness? What is it? What should it be?

*****

A Happy Day Commitment Chart

<table>
<tr><td>Rocking Start of the Day (First 15 minutes)</td><td><ul><li>Be thankfull for still being alive</li><li>Make my bed</li><li>Meditation for 5 minutes.</li></ul></td></tr>
<tr><td>Workout
Breakfast</td><td rowspan="5"><ul><li>To take few minutes off to do some fun stuff… a few deep breaths, 1-minute meditation, just a walk, listen to a song.</li><li>Stay focused on what is really important or urgent and save time for yourself for what really matters for your happiness.</li><li>Any stress/failure situation, after you have done what you could do, get your learning from it, and let it go. It will also pass. Just take a deep breath, laugh and move on.</li></ul></td></tr>
<tr><td>Classes</td></tr>
<tr><td>Lunch</td></tr>
<tr><td>Classes/Assignments</td></tr>
<tr><td>After Classes fun time & reading
(friends, dinner, late night campus walks)</td></tr>
<tr><td>Smiling Closure of the Day (Last 15 minutes)</td><td><ul><li>Write my gratitude diary.</li><li>5-minute meditation.</li><li>Smile.</li></ul></td></tr>
</table>

*****

Next day, in the evening after dinner, over a walk in the campus.

Nitish: Good, finally I am implementing the strategy for the path to happiness.

Eva: That's great.

Surender: What is your resource allocation for the strategy.

Varun: Why to worry, allocate as you go along.

Surender: No that's a way to disaster. You should have some formula for resource allocation to support the chosen strategy.

Ekta: Yes, it makes sense.

Nitish: Yes, I agree and I do have a formula. I am going to spend 50 percent of resources on work, 25 percent on health, 15 percent on relationships and 5 percent each on philanthropy and spirituality/ religion.

Manoj: Yes, that looks good.

Resource Allocation

Resource Allocation: Choosing a strategy in itself is of no use if proper resource allocation is not done to support the chosen strategy.

Application in the story: Nitish is giving 50 percent of resources to work, 25 percent to health, 15 percent to relationships, and 5 percent each to philanthropy and spirituality/religion. This is resource allocation.

It's your turn now: Have you done resource allocation for Happiness? How are you ensuring proper resource allocation? How should you improve it further?

*****

A few days later, during lunch hours.

Ekta: Where is Nitish?

Varun: He is still in gym. He has got inspired by the bodybuilder trainer and other body builder students and is there all the time.

Ekta: Wow! So he is going to be a body building champion now?

Eva: Looks like he has gone off the track.

Surender: Yes, that's not good for his happiness strategy. Someone needs to talk to him.

Manoj: Ha-ha, he has fallen into the growth trap!

Growth Trap

Growth Trap: Even after choosing a strategy, organizations are lured into mindless growth for which they deviate from the chosen strategy and that creates trouble.

Application in the story: Nitish needs to give some time to gym but there he saw these group of bodybuilder students and trainer and fell for bodybuilding, ignoring his overall happiness strategy. This is a growth trap.

It's your turn now: Have you fallen into growth trap for Happiness? How are you ensuring avoiding the growth trap? How should you avoid it?

*****

Later in the night over coffee in the canteen.

Surender: How is everything going with you Nitish?

Nitish: All is going great so far! I am enjoying the gym and see my biceps are shaping up.

Eva: That's good. What about other things?

Nitish: Yes, I am going to work on other parts of the body too.

Surender: She is not asking about that. Forget it. What about your five dimensional happiness? How is it going? Do you still remember it?

Nitish: Oh, OMG. Yes, I got it. Both of you are trying to remind me of that path to happiness.

Surender: Yes, you need to stay focused and have the discipline to stick to it. Otherwise it is of no use. It would stay on a piece of paper.

Eva: You have worked a lot on developing that document on the path to happiness. You should not throw it away like that.

Nitish: Sorry, I got carried away in the gym.

Surender: Good. Do everything in a balanced way and follow your dreams.

Focus & Discipline

Focus & Discipline: These suggest that once the organization has chosen a particular strategy, it needs to stay focused and disciplined on implementing it.

Application in the story: Nitish realizes his mistake of not staying focused and disciplined in implementing the strategy for path to happiness.

It's your turn now: Are you staying focused on your Happiness strategy? How are you ensuring the discipline and focus on the strategy? How you should do it?

*****

A few days later, over breakfast in the hostel mess.

Nitish: It is all so easy to say go for meditation but so difficult to follow it. I am not able to do it. Within a few seconds my mind goes after this or that thought. I try to bring it back to focus, but again it goes away after another thought. It is so frustrating.

Eva: Yes, it is not easy. It is very difficult in the beginning. Maybe you are trying it in wrong way.

Nitish: I am focusing on my breath but all sort of ideas keep coming and my mind keeps wandering all around and I give it up after a while.

Eva: Oh, Ok. You need to give it another try.

Execution Troubles

Execution Troubles: There are some problems an organizations faces while implementing a strategy and these are called execution troubles.

Application in the story: Nitish is trying to apply his path to happiness strategy and one part of it is mediation. It is new for him and he is facing trouble in implementing it. These are called execution troubles in strategy.

It's your turn now: What are your execution issues? How are you solving these issues? How should you do it?

*****

After dinner, over a walk in the campus.

There is a fight going on between Varun and Nitish. Nitish and Varun were participating in a startup competition and Nitish made a silly mistake and they lost the competition.

Varun: You are such an idiot. How can you make such a dumb mistake?

Nitish: Oh look who is talking. Why did not you tell me the details before the final round of competition?

Varun: It was a mistake to take you in my team.

Eva: Enough, both of you stop now. Varun you have started three startups and so you know all, and almost anything on startups looks obvious to you. It's not the same with Nitish. You should have explained to him in detail rather than assuming he also knows as you know.

Surender: Varun, this is a classic example of curse of knowledge.

Manoj: Yes, that's so true. Professor Doordarshi was damn right about it. Now I understand why curse of knowledge is one of the reasons behind strategy not being well understood in the organizations as the top management assumes that everyone in the organization is at the same level of understanding and knowledge and things are explained in an abstract way which remain beyond understanding for many in the organization! I myself have witnessed it in my last organization.

Curse of Knowledge

Curse of Knowledge: Assuming everyone is at same level of understanding or knowledge as you are and then not explaining things in details and properly.

Application in the story: Varun assumed that Nitish knows and understands about startups as much as he does. This leads to him not explaining many things in detail to Nitish. This is the curse of knowledge.

It's your turn now: Are you facing a curse of knowledge for happiness strategy? How are you solving these issues? How should you do it?

*****

In the afternoon, in the office of strategy Professor Husmukh Doordarshi.

Professor Doordarshi: You don't look happy to me. How is your path to happiness journey going so far?

Nitish: You are right. I am finding it difficult. I am not happy. It is so difficult to implement and results are so slow.

Professor Doordarshi: Ha-ha. It's a case of misplaced assumptions!

Nitish: What do you mean?

Professor Doordarshi: Look, why did you assume it is going to be easy? Why did you assume the results are going to be fast?

Nitish: Just like that. I assumed so.

Professor Doordarshi: That's the problem. It is one of fundamental problem in happiness. People make all kind of assumptions without knowing whether these are right or wrong assumptions. And then wonder why are they not happy? It is same in strategy.

Nitish: Yes, I see your point.

Professor Doordarshi: You need to be realistic with assumptions. Assumptions should be real.

Nitish: Yes, I made a blunder. From now onwards I am going to be realistic with assumptions.

Importance of Assumptions

Assumptions: For the success of any strategy, making the right assumptions on which the strategy is based is very important. If assumptions are wrong, the strategy will fail.

Application in the story: Nitish has made assumptions just like that without thinking much and now he is finding things difficult. This shows the importance of assumptions.

It's your turn now: What are your assumptions for Happiness? Are they correct? Do you keep checking your assumptions for Happiness?

*****

Over an evening walk.

Eva: Why Varun looks so upset today.

Ekta: Don't tell me. You don't know? You must be kidding!

Eva: Yes, I have no idea. I swear.

Ekta: It is hilarious and sad too. He goes to this yoga classes just outside our campus gate. He was thinking of proposing to one of the girls there for some time but yesterday one of our classmates proposed to her first and she said yes. So he was just thinking and analyzing and planning all the while, and someone else just did it and he is mad at himself about it.

Eva: Ha ha. That's a classic case of paralysis by analysis.

Paralysis by Analysis

Paralysis by Analysis: This means some analysis is required but it is more important to take a decision and act otherwise you would be still analyzing and someone else will run away with the customers!

Application in the story: While Varun is still getting more information about the girl and analyzing it, someone else proposes to her and she accepts. Varun needed to do some analysis but it was more important to take a decision and act. This is paralysis by analysis.

It's your turn now: Have you faced paralysis by analysis in your search for Happiness? How are you taking care of it? How should you take care of it?

*****

After some time, in the evening walk.

Eva: BTW, have you made any progress in finding a partner?

Ekta: I was not making much progress by depending on my friends' network. After one bad incident, I don't trust relatives anymore. A few weeks back, I got on these matrimonial and dating platforms and I think these are good.

Eva: Great! So we can hear some good news soon.

Ekta: I think; I was already applying what these Professors are teaching me now! That is a platform strategy I am following. I mean I am a consumer in these platforms and I am using the power of platforms to reach out to a larger audience for a potential alliance. And I can leave any platform whenever I want.

Eva: Yes, you are so ahead of Professor Doordarshi! Ha-ha!

Platform Strategy

Platform Strategy: Platforms are places like Amazon, Google etc. where suppliers and consumers meet. As an organization you need to decide on creating your own platform or be a part of some other platform and how to play there.

Application in the story: Ekta's platform strategy is to be part of these platforms and use the power of the platform to reach out to a larger audience for a potential alliance.

It's your turn now: What is your platform strategy for Happiness? Is it correct? What it should be?

*****

Over dinner in the hostel mess.

Ekta: Where is Nitish today?

Varun: He has gone to meet some monk with someone from the class.

Eva: That's a good thing he is doing. The poor guy needs some peace of mind. It is not easy to implement strategy on oneself.

Manoj: Yes, it is not so easy.

Surender: Maybe I should also try it sometime.

Ekta: Yes, I might join you if it is for a short duration and somewhere nearby.

Surender: Ok, I will let you know.

Strategic Alignment

Strategic Alignment: It means that all activities of an organization should be aligned with the chosen strategy of the organisation.

Application in the story: Nitish is trying to undertake activities in line with his path to happiness. Spirituality is one of the dimensions of happiness and he has gone to explore it by going to meet some monk. This is called strategic alignment.

It's your turn now: Are your activities aligned with your Happiness strategy? What are you doing for strategic alignment? What should you be doing for it?

*****

A few days later. It is 26th Jan which is a national festival in India and a big parade is organized in the capital city, New Delhi. It is an extended holiday and many students have gone home.

Varun is roaming around aimlessly on the hostel rooftop.

Varun has this crazy habit of taking aims with stones. His second attempt is always on target.

He picks up a small stone and targets a nearby street lamp but misses the target. He picks up a much bigger stone. He sees a monkey with his back towards him. Out of nowhere he throws the stone towards the monkey casually. And it hits the monkey! The monkey goes crazy and runs after him. Varun takes the stairs to escape the monkey but the monkey is running after him, he jumps 3-4 stairs in one go and reaches the top floor of the hostel and the monkey is after him making loud strange sounds and they keep running on that floor for some time till Varun finds an open door and rushes inside the room and closes it from inside. But the monkey stays there for some time.

This is witnessed by some students including Nitish who were on the other side of the top floor. They all burst out in loud laughter, saying it serves him right for his crazy habits!

Next day, over lunch break, in the hostel mess. The group is laughing about it as they have come to know about it.

Ekta: What is wrong with you Varun?

Varun: It just happened.

Eva: Thank God, you are safe today.

Manoj: You should be careful, Varun.

Varun: *(To change the topic)* Where is Nitish today?

Manoj: He has taken up some live project where he is getting a good stipend too.

Surender: That's good. He is trying to spend money on philanthropy and that's a good way to make some quick bucks.

Entrepreneurship

Entrepreneurship: It is about creating new ventures.

Application in the story: Nitish needs money to spend on philanthropy and he takes up some new live project to make some money. This is called entrepreneurship.

It's your turn now: Do you have an entrepreneurship strategy for Happiness? What is it? What should it be?

*****

Rohit, the crazy student, is nicknamed 'one question wonder' by his classmates. He has this habit of asking one question in each class! And that's his way of getting his return on investment i.e. focused attention for 3-5 minutes of the class time. But most of his questions are too obvious or stupid at times.

In the marketing class.

The Professor was telling about an upcoming exam for the class. And he has explained everything in detail.

Professor: Your end of term exam is an open book exam.

Rohit: You mean it is not a closed book exam?

Professor: *(a bit irritated)* Yes, that is what I mean. *(And after a quick pause, with a smile)* But if you are going to miss it, I can arrange a closed book exam for you!

Class laughs out loud.

And a whispering noise says, yes sir, please do it for him.

After the class in the institute canteen for lunch.

Eva: Manoj, you are looking fitter these days.

Manoj: Yes, I am trying.

Ekta: What you mean by trying? You are so much into anything related to fitness and healthy living these days.

Nitish: I saw; you have started juggling these days.

Varun: Yes, I saw you yesterday juggling with jogging.

Manoj: Yes, it's fun. I am scared of water but there are so many benefits of swimming. So to fix that, I thought of some similar exercise and I ended up with combining juggling with jogging.

Eva: That's a good innovation for you.

Surender: Good going, keep it up!

Innovation

Innovation: Innovation is something new which creates commercial or social value or both.

Application in the story: Manoj is combining juggling with jogging. This is called innovation.

It's your turn now: Do you have an innovation strategy for Happiness? What is it? What should it be?

*****

A few days later, it is end of term exams.

The students were so happy to see the question paper for the end term examination for marketing. The question paper was the same as the midterm examination question paper. Everyone is smiling and a bit surprised also, but they don't say a word about it and answer the questions.

After the examination.

Varun: The Professor has told us the end term paper would be very similar to the mid-term paper, but good to see it exactly the same.

Ekta: Yes, it was fun.

Suriender: Maybe it is a mistake.

Next day the Professor got to know about this and realized his mistake. He apologized for this mistake in a mail and arranged a repeat examination.

Same day, over lunch, in the hostel canteen.

Surender: Hey, how are your preparations going for the final round of competition.

Nitish: I am trying to crack it but not sure.

Ekta: You will make it. You have already made it to the final round of the competition and you are the only one from India. This is an international competition among management students organized by a Fortune 500 company named HAHA. It is a big achievement.

Varun: Don't forget, it is happening in NewYork. You are getting a free ticket and a week's accommodation there. If you win, you get a prize of USD 10,000.

Manoj: Yes, it is a good exposure for you.

Eva: Don't take stress. You stay focused and you can win it, I am sure.

Nitish: I am trying to stay calm and focused.

International Strategy

International Strategy: It is the strategy of an organization involved in business in more than one country for dealing with international business.

Application in the story: Nitish is participating in an international competition on developing a tag line for a MNC. This is international strategy.

It's your turn now: Do you have an international strategy for Happiness? What is it? What should it be?

*****

Later that night. In the hostel room.

Nitish: I am not sure how should I prepare for the stay and presentations for the competition in New York.

Manoj: What is the confusion?

Nitish: Should I try to go the Indian way or be more American or just a normal international style.

Manoj: Since it is an international competition, I suggest you go the international way and don't try to overdo anything either Indian or American.

Varun: Yes, carry your normal formal dresses and stay in normal international youth hostels to save money.

Transnational Model

Transnational Model: When organizations go international there are pressures to be locally responsive, and pressure to reduce cost. When an organization is reducing cost and is also locally responsive, then it is called transnational strategy.

Application in the story: The Transanational Strategy for Nitish is given below

Pressure to reduce cost		Low	High
	High	Same standardized style	Adapt but with low cost
	Low	No change, go as it.	Adapt with high cost.
		Low	High
		Pressure to adapt	

It's your turn now: Do you have a transnational strategy for Happiness? What is it? What should it be?

*****

It is last day of the end of term examination.

After the Accounting exam, over coffee in the evening in the Institute canteen., Varun and Ekta are fighting. And Eva asks why are they fighting.

Ekta: This Varun is impossible.

Today after one hour in the exam, I heard someone's snoring from behind. I ignored it and tried to resume writing answers thinking the snoring will stop. It continued for the next 10 minutes when I started pitying the person behind me. With 2 invigilators in the room, I finally dared to look back. I saw it was Varun who was sleeping on the answer sheet with pen in hand. The tip of the pen was touching the answer sheet with a big blot of ink on the paper.

I shook him and he finally woke up. But the invigilator saw me looking behind and immediately shouted from the other corner to stop and ran towards me as if she had caught me cheating. I explained the situation but the invigilator didn't believe. I then showed the ink blot to prove Varun was sleeping and I had just woken him up and not cheated.

Still the invigilator gave me a warning before she went away.

Varun: I did not sleep at all last night and don't know somehow I fell asleep after seeing the boring questions.

After few sips of coffee.

Eva: I admire Nitish for the way he carries himself. Varun you should learn from him.

Ekta: Yes, I find him quite transparent, accountable and fair with us.

Manoj: He is same with his family too.

Surender: That's great.

Varun: But it must be quite boring, maybe.

Ekta: Please leave the poor soul alone. You are always pulling his leg.

Eva: Yes, I agree with this.

Varun: Oh, come on. I do this just to make him relax a bit more.

Corporate Governance

Corporate Governance: It refers to how the organization is governed and run. The most important components are transparency, accountability and fairness.

Application in the story: Nitish is quite transparent, accountable and fair in his dealings. This is a corporate governance.

It's your turn now: Do you have corporate governance strategy for Happiness? What is it? What should it be?

*****

After a guest session. On the way back from the auditorium to the hostel.

Nitish: I am so impressed by the guest speaker today. He is so right in saying that leadership is about being a good teacher too for your followers.

Surender: You bet. He is so on the mark.

Nitish: I am going to volunteer teaching teachers in the school next door to our campus on management lessons.

Eva: That's smart move.

Ekta: Yes, it is a win-win situation for both the parties.

Strategic Corporate Social Responsibility (CSR)

Strategic CSR: Strategic CSR is not philanthropy. Strategic CSR is done in such a way that it helps the organization as well as the receiver of it.

Application in the story: Nitish is going to harness his leadership skills by training the teachers and teachers will learn about management lessons. This is called strategic CSR.

It's your turn now: Do you have a strategic CSR for Happiness? What is it? What should it be?

*****

A few days later, in the afternoon. In the office of Professor Husmukh.

Nitish: Professor, I am totally lost on the organizational structure part. How can one have an organizational structure for himself?

Professor Doordarshi: Go to the reason why structure is needed?

Nitish: I guess it is for better organization of work and accountability and control.

Professor Doordarshi: To achieve your path to happiness, can you do it all alone?

Nitish: No, I need to work with others.

Professor Doordarshi: So can you try some kind of organizational structure?

Nitish: Let me try. There are no direct full time employees in this case. But there are people with whom I need to work to achieve my path to happiness such as the trainer in the gym, the monk in the temple, and so on. So a loose entrepreneurial structure is my solution?

Organizational Structure

Organizational Structure: The various activities in an organization are arranged into departments and the whole organization is arranged in a hierarchy with roles and responsibilities. This is called a structure.

Application in the story: There are no direct full time employees in this case. This kind of structure can be loosely called as an entrepreneurial structure.

It's your turn now: Do you have an organizational structure for Happiness strategy? What is it? What should it be?

*****

A few days later.

There is a readymade garment shop near the institute gate and it always shows a signboard saying 50 percent sale and today is the last day of the sale.

Varun, Ekta and Nitish are passing by it. Varun stops them and ask them to join him in the shop.

Shopkeeper: Yes, please, may I show you the items on sale? Today is the last day of the sale.

Varun: Oh, ok. Let me go through the items.

After 5 minutes.

Varun: I like these five items.

Shopkeeper: After discount, you need to pay INR 2000.

Varun: Looking in all his pockets. Oh, but I have not brought my wallet today.

Ekta and Nitish play along and say they have already spent their money and are left with just the taxi fare.

Varun looks very sad and dejected.

Varun: (*In a pleading voice*) I really like the stuff here but today I don't have sufficient money. I am going to come back tomorrow. Please keep the sale for one more day or allow me to use this sale price for just one more day.

Shopkeeper: (*In a very firm voice*) The sale is for today only. Why don't you use some online payment method?

Varun: (*Sheepishly*) Sorry, we don't know how to use those online methods. We are from small faraway places and are new to this big city.

Shopkeeper: (*In an irritated but boastful voice*) Ok, I can keep this special price only for you and only for one more day.

Varun: (*Looking relaxed and happy*) Thank you so much. You are like a big brother to me. I will come back tomorrow morning. Please keep these five items for me.

The others also look happy and thank the shopkeeper.

They leave the shop.

After some meters away from the shop, all of them burst out in loud laughter.

In the evening, after dinner.

Nitish: I am not sure if all my strategy pieces are together.

Manoj: Why don't you go for a reality check. Let's do it now for you.

Eva: Yes, it is a good idea. Your strategy for happiness is through a combination of growth strategies at a corporate level.

Varun: Structure is loosely entrepreneurial.

Ekta: You have put routines and habits in place which takes care of the systems part.

Manoj: And your goal is to be happy and stay happy.

Surender: Your skills include both hard (e.g. analysis) and soft skills (e. g. resource management, time management)

Eva: And your style is participatory.

Manoj: And it all looks good together. You are unnecessarily worried.

McKinsey 7S Framework

McKinsey 7S Framework: It is a framework to access and ensure that strategy, structure, systems, super ordinate goals, skills, staff and style of organization fit together in a mutually supportive way for good performance.

Application in the story: McKinsey 7S framework is given below.

7S Component	For Nitish
Strategy	Path to happiness through a combination of growth and stability strategies at corporate level.
Structure	Entrepreneurial structure
Systems	Routines in place
Super ordinate Goals	Happiness
Skills	Soft skills (such as time management, resource allocation) and hard skills (such as analysis).
Staff	No direct staff. Friends act as support.
Style	Participatory

It's your turn now: Do you have a McKinsey 7S framework for Happiness? What is it? What should it be?

*****

After dinner, on the rooftop of the hostel.

Varun: How is your philanthropy part going Nitish.

Nitish: I started without a clear idea but it has turned out to be pretty satisfying.

When I started I had no idea about it. But after discussion with Professor Doordarshi I made a beginning. Over time I have increased my earnings to spend more on philanthropy. So my strategy has emerged over time.

Surender: That's a good start I must appreciate.

Ekta: Yes, he has been able to crack it.

Nitish: And Eva has always been quite helpful with her insights on this.

Eva: Well you are a quick learner.

Emergent Strategy

Emergent Strategy: The idea that when an organization looks back and identifies how its strategy has emerged over a time period is called emergent strategy. It is opposite of the thought that the firm always starts with a well defined strategy and sticks to it.

Application in the story: Nitish has no idea about philanthropy and his ideas and strategy started after discussions with Professor Doordarshi and he kept working on it with time. This way his strategy has emerged and that's called emergent strategy.

It's your turn now: Do you have an emergent strategy for Happiness? How has your strategy for Happiness has emerged? How it should have emerged?

*****

It is four months into the MBA program. Late in the evening, Nitish is reflecting over the past four months.

It has been an interesting journey so far. I have made real progress on my path to happiness both in terms of formulating the strategy and implementing it. It is going well so far....... I am able to score well in mid - term exams and have got a few live projects too. .... These five new friends are a good addition to my list of friends as they are quite supportive and experienced also.

His mind keeps wandering till he gets a phone call from home.

*****

Happiness Masterclass 7

Create tools to measure progress on happiness and feedback.

Happiness is both a journey and destination and one needs to stay on the right path.

Keep simple checks and balances to make sure you are following your path to happiness and you are happy now.

Part VII

Evaluation Of Happiness

Time flies. It is the end of 9 months of the MBA program.

In the middle of the placement week.

In the institute cafeteria, over a coffee.

Ekta: You are impossible Varun.

Varun: It is not my mistake. I was sent to the wrong room.

Ekta: You should have kept your eyes open and looked at the signboards.

Varun: The placement committee should have not done it.

Eva: What happened. Why are you fighting?

Ekta: Varun was preparing for a marketing role in company X but ended up in the room for the rival company Y for a finance interview and he screwed big time as he starting telling about why he loves marketing and how much eager he is to join the marketing team of company X!

Nitish: And one of the interviewers started laughing while other got angry about this comedy of errors! That kind of created a funny and awkward scene there!

Manoj: But the good news is, he got back to his scenes fast and cracked the interview when he went to the correct room after some time.

Ekta: But it is going to be remembered for a long time! A classic case of a comedy of errors! And who better than Varun to be a part of it! Ha Ha.

Next day, in the late night, in Institute canteen.

Ekta: OMG, it was unbelievable.

Eva: Yes, I have heard about it. But tell us in detail as you were part of it.

Ekta: There was this group discussion taking place for the placement process. An advertisement was being shown and students had to discuss that advertisement and also tell the product for which that advertisement was made along with the reasons. One student started, followed by another student followed by replies from two other students, and consequently, two groups of five each were having two simultaneous discussions on the same topic which was supposed to be discussion of one whole group of the ten students. This was a hilarious scene for everyone and the moderator was frustrated and pleaded and scolded simultaneously to stop the discussion. When the results came, the whole panel group was scrapped.

Nitish: Oh, that's crazy.

Ekta: Crazy it was. You should have been there to see it!

Placement week has just got over. It is Saturday evening and the group is in a beer café in cyber hub.

Varun: Wow! I am so happy! We all made it, finally! Cheers!!!

Everyone says cheers.

Ekta: Yes, it is great! Hurray!!! I can't believe we all got our dream jobs! Cheers to all of us!!!

Cheers to all of us, everyone says.

Nitish: I am going to drink and dance all night! Who else is joining me?

Silence.

Nitish looks confused.

All others break in loud laughter and say yes!!!

Eva: We should party till we can't stand on our legs!!!

Varun: And who so ever falls first is going to pay the bills!!!

All say yes.

Manoj: After the pub closes here, we move to my place and that party is on me.

All say yes.

And they keep drinking and talking and dancing all night.

*****

It is a day before the Institute convocation ceremony.

In the office of Professor Husmukh Doordarshi.

Professor Doordarshi: So Nitish, how would you evaluate yourself on your path to happiness?

Nitish: I think I have done reasonably well.

I got good grades and got the placement I was looking for.

My health has improved and I developed biceps too.

I am much closer to my family and friends now.

I am enjoying the time and efforts spent in philanthropy and on religion/spirituality.

More than all this, now I am happy and can stay happy.

Professor Doordarshi: Great! I am happy to see you making so much progress.

Nitish: And it has not been possible without your regular guidance and feedback. Thanks a lot.

Professor Doordarshi: Nope its mainly due to your efforts. But now the challenge is to stay focused on this journey of happiness and stay happy.

Nitish: I think I can manage this now.

Professor Doordarshi: Good luck than for your convocation tomorrow!

Balanced Scorecard

Balanced Scorecard: It is a comprehensive tool to evaluate performance. It consists of four parts namely financial perspective, customer perspective, internal process perspective and learning & growth perspective.

Application in the story: Balance scorecard from Nitish's perspective is given below.

Balanced Scorecard Component	**For Nitish**
Financial Perspective	He got good grades and good placement.
Customer Perspective	His Professor Husmukh Doordarshis, industry, friends and family look satisfied with him.
Internal Process Perspective	He has developed new habits and that has helped him.
Learning & Growth Perspective	His learning and development have been good and looks like it is going to continue so.

It's your turn now: Do you have a balance scorecard for Happiness? What is it? What should it be?

*****

Next day, just before convocation. On the Institute lawn outside the convocation hall.

Professor Doordarshi: By the way, one more thing you need to remember.

This time, everything has fallen in place as you have desired through your strategy, but it is not always like this. There are instances of strategy failure too and you should be open to that. Strategy has its limitations too. One of its limitation is it is too much focused on analysis and there is a need to balance it with more application of intuition too.

Nitish: OK! I am going to take note of this.

Limitations of Strategy

Limitations of strategy: As in life, so in strategy, there is no guarantee of success. Strategy has its limitations and there is a need for both analysis and intuition in strategy.

Application in the story: In this case, strategy has worked well for Nitish till now.

It's your turn now: Are you aware of limitations of your strategy for Happiness? How are you managing it? How you should manage it?

*****

Everyone enters and takes their positions for convocation in the auditorium.

A mild earthquake is noticed.

The group bursts in loud laughter.

Ekta: This is nothing.

Manoj: Yes, it is nothing. I am sure; we all still remember our Earthquake experience from our trip in the long weekend last week.

Eva: Yes, that was really funny.

And they all somehow went in a reflecting mood for few seconds.

Varun vividly remembers the scene in the hotel room for the trip. It was around 9 am and he got up and went to washroom. In the washroom while he was brushing his teeth, he noticed his legs were wavering.

Manoj (to himself): Hey, looks like the hangover is still not gone. Why my legs are wavering, that's strange!

Oh, no, even the ceiling fan is oscillating! My head has really gone crazy with the hangover.

At that very moment, there is a loud knock on the door and Varun and Nitish are heard shouting it is an earthquake! Run out of building!

Manoj runs out of the door in his towel and runs through the stairs and see the other five already going ahead of him. He noticed two people standing casually by the stairs and looking amusingly at them. They reach outside the building in the open. But to their surprise, they see no one else outside. They later figured out earthquakes are so common in the city.

There is an announcement from the stage for the beginning of the proceedings for the convocation and their mind comes back to the current situation.

After the convocation.

Varun: Finally, it's over. I am so happy.

Ekta: Yes, we got decent grades and jobs of our choices.

Manoj: Yes, I also got time to regain my lost health here and that's great.

Eva: And Nitish, you have more or less achieved all in your path to happiness strategy. And we also learned a lot from your experiences.

Nitish: Yes, things have fallen in place. You all have been a great support and fun.

Surender: It's great to see all of us getting more or less of what we came for here. It has been a great experience.

Varun: And finally, it's time to say goodbye for now as our taxis are waiting for us.

They hug each other and leave for their destinations. It's a new journey and new path to happiness.

*****

References

The strategy concepts explained in the book are given by number of Professors and some practitioners and these are available in any standard strategy book such as:

Hitt, M. A., Ireland, R. D., & Hoskisson, R. E. (2012). *Strategic management cases: competitiveness and globalization*. Cengage Learning.

Osterwalder, A., & Pigneur, Y. (2010). *Business model generation: a handbook for visionaries, game changers, and challengers*. John Wiley & Sons.

The glossary of MBA jargons and the happiness workbook are a modification of the same used in my earlier book Love Strategy.

The brief explanation of some of the concepts are taken from my earlier book Love Strategy.

Annexure I

Concept of Minimum Viable Happiness (let's call it as Working Definition of Happiness)

Minimum viable happiness means lack of stress due to any major trouble in the five areas of life namely, professional success, personal relationships, health, philanthropy, and spirituality/religion.

Annexure II

Glossary of MBA Jargons

Assignment: Work to be done by students on an individual or group basis and submitted to the Professor.

Case Study: An extract of a company experience (real or created) to explain management concepts.

Case Analysis: Analysis of a case study to understand the underlying management concepts.

Case Competition: Inter-institute case study competition

Convocation: Degree awarding ceremony.

Final placement: Getting a job in a company during the last few months of the course completion of MBA course. Companies visit the institute and conduct interviews for selection.

Grade: Marks scored in exams.

Group Project: While doing an MBA, a group project requires a group of students to work on a topic given by the faculty.

Live Project: While doing an MBA, working on a management topic given by a company for a few months/weeks primarily to gain hands on experience.

Term: A one year MBA program is of four terms and each term is of three months' duration.

Mid-term Exam: Performance evaluation for an individual student after completion of half a term which is of three months.

End-term Exam: Performance evaluation for an individual student after completion of half a term which is of three months.

Annexure III

A Happy Day Commitment Chart

Rocking Start of the Day (First 15 minutes)	• Be thankfull for still being alive • Make your bed • Meditation for 5 minutes.
Workout/yoga/sports Breakfast	• Don't forget to take few minutes off to do some fun stuff…may be a dart game in your office, a few deep breaths, 1-minute meditation, just a walk, listen to a song, grab a good drink. • Stay focused on what is really important or urgent and save time for yourself for what really matters for your happiness. • Any stress/failure situation, after you have done what you could do, get your learning from it, and let it go. It will also pass. Just take a deep breath, laugh and move on.
Work	
Lunch	
Work	
After work fun time in gym/family/friends/ sports/ dinner	
Smiling Closure of the Day (Last 15 minutes)	• Write your gratitude diary. • 5-minute meditation. • Smile.

Annexure IV

Strategy Document for the Path to Happiness

<table>
<tr><td colspan="5">Vision</td></tr>
<tr><td colspan="5">Mission</td></tr>
<tr><td colspan="5">Core Values</td></tr>
<tr><td colspan="5">Corporate Level Strategy</td></tr>
<tr><td>Work</td><td>Health</td><td>Relationships</td><td>Religion/
Spirituality</td><td>Philanthropy</td></tr>
<tr><td></td><td></td><td></td><td></td><td></td></tr>
<tr><td colspan="5">Business Level Strategy</td></tr>
<tr><td>Work</td><td>Health</td><td>Relationships</td><td>Religion/
Spirituality</td><td>Philanthropy</td></tr>
<tr><td></td><td></td><td></td><td></td><td></td></tr>
</table>

Annexure V

Happiness Workbook

<table>
<tr><td colspan="5">Workbook
(To see where do you stand in happiness strategy)
Note: While answering the questions, your focus should remain on achieving your desired vision through your happiness strategy.</td></tr>
<tr><td rowspan="2">Sr. No</td><td rowspan="2">Variable</td><td colspan="3">Response</td></tr>
<tr><td>Yes</td><td>No</td><td>Not Applicable</td></tr>
<tr><td rowspan="4">1</td><td colspan="4">Art of Asking Questions</td></tr>
<tr><td>Do you ask good questions for happiness ?</td><td></td><td></td><td></td></tr>
<tr><td colspan="4">What are your questions ?</td></tr>
<tr><td colspan="4">What should they be?</td></tr>
<tr><td rowspan="4">2</td><td colspan="4">Art of Framing a Problem</td></tr>
<tr><td colspan="4">How are you framing your problem of happiness?</td></tr>
<tr><td colspan="4">Is it correct?</td></tr>
<tr><td colspan="4">What should it be?</td></tr>
<tr><td rowspan="4">3</td><td colspan="4">Art of Structured Thinking</td></tr>
<tr><td>Do you apply structured thinking for happiness?</td><td></td><td></td><td></td></tr>
<tr><td colspan="4">Is it correct ?</td></tr>
<tr><td colspan="4">What should it be?</td></tr>
</table>

<table>
<tr><td rowspan="4">4</td><td colspan="4">Vision</td></tr>
<tr><td>Do you have a vision for happiness?</td><td></td><td></td><td></td></tr>
<tr><td>Is it the right one for you?</td><td></td><td></td><td></td></tr>
<tr><td colspan="4">What should it be?</td></tr>
<tr><td rowspan="4">5</td><td colspan="4">Mission</td></tr>
<tr><td>Do you have a mission for happiness?</td><td></td><td></td><td></td></tr>
<tr><td>Is it the right one for you?</td><td></td><td></td><td></td></tr>
<tr><td colspan="4">What should it be?</td></tr>
<tr><td rowspan="4">6</td><td colspan="4">Core Values</td></tr>
<tr><td>Do you have core values?</td><td></td><td></td><td></td></tr>
<tr><td>Do your core values come in way for finding happiness or maintain happiness ?</td><td></td><td></td><td></td></tr>
<tr><td colspan="4">What should they be?</td></tr>
</table>

7	External Environment Analysis PEST Analysis			
	Have you done a PEST analysis for finding happiness or maintaining existing happiness?			
	Are you managing it?			
	How you should manage it?			

8	Industry Environment Analysis			
	Have you done a five force analysis for finding happiness or maintaining happiness ?			
	Is it favorable?			
	How can you manage it better?			
9	Internal Environment Analysis			
	Have you done an internal analysis for finding or maintaining happiness?			
	Is it favorable?			
	How can you manage it better?			

10	Core Competence			
	What is your core competency for finding or maintaining happiness?			
	Are these sufficient?			
	How are you making sure you nourish yourself and add more core competencies?			
11	SWOT analysis			
	Have you done a SWOT analysis for finding or maintaining happiness?			
	Is it favorable?			
	How can you manage it better?			
12	Competitive Advantage			
	What is your competitive advantage for finding happiness or maintaining happiness?			
	Is it sufficient?			
	How are you improving it?			

<table>
<tr><td rowspan="4">13</td><td colspan="4">Value Addition</td></tr>
<tr><td colspan="4">What is your value addition to your happiness?</td></tr>
<tr><td>Is it sufficient?</td><td></td><td></td><td></td></tr>
<tr><td colspan="4">How are you improving it?</td></tr>
</table>

<table>
<tr><td rowspan="4">14</td><td colspan="4">Value Chain Analysis</td></tr>
<tr><td>Have you done a value chain for your new or existing happiness?</td><td></td><td></td><td></td></tr>
<tr><td colspan="4">What are the activities you need to remove?</td></tr>
<tr><td colspan="4">What are the activities you should focus on more?</td></tr>
</table>

15	Strategic Alternatives and Choice
	Which dimension of professional success happiness are you currently focused on?
	What are your alternatives?
	Which one you should focus on?

16	Strategy Levels
	What is your overall strategy for happiness?
	What is your strategy for professional success happiness?
	What is your strategy for managing time and finances, your friends, managing meetings, image etc. for happiness?

17	Cost Leadership Strategy			
	Are you following a cost leadership strategy?			
	What is your cost leadership strategy?			
	What should it be?			

18	Differentiation Strategy			
	Are you following a differentiation strategy?			
	What is your differentiation strategy?			
	What should it be?			

<table>
<tr><td rowspan="4">19</td><td colspan="4">Niche Strategy</td></tr>
<tr><td>Are you following a niche strategy?</td><td></td><td></td><td></td></tr>
<tr><td colspan="4">What is your niche strategy?</td></tr>
<tr><td colspan="4">What should it be?</td></tr>
</table>

<table>
<tr><td rowspan="4">20</td><td colspan="4">Strategy</td></tr>
<tr><td>Do you have a strategy for finding or maintaining happiness?</td><td></td><td></td><td></td></tr>
<tr><td colspan="4">What is your strategy for happiness?</td></tr>
<tr><td colspan="4">What should it be?</td></tr>
</table>

<table>
<tr><td rowspan="4">21</td><td colspan="4">Tactics</td></tr>
<tr><td colspan="4">What are the tactics you have for happiness?</td></tr>
<tr><td>Do these help in strategy?</td><td></td><td></td><td></td></tr>
<tr><td colspan="4">What should your tactics be ?</td></tr>
<tr><td rowspan="4">22</td><td colspan="4">BCG matrix</td></tr>
<tr><td>Do you have a BCG matrix for happiness?</td><td></td><td></td><td></td></tr>
<tr><td colspan="4">What is it?</td></tr>
<tr><td colspan="4">What should it be?</td></tr>
<tr><td rowspan="4">23</td><td colspan="4">Diversification (Ansoff Matrix)</td></tr>
<tr><td>Do you have an Ansoff matrix for happiness?</td><td></td><td></td><td></td></tr>
<tr><td colspan="4">What is it?</td></tr>
<tr><td colspan="4">What should it be?</td></tr>
</table>

24	Strategic Alliances			
	Do you have a strategic alliance for happiness?			
	What is it?			
	What should it be?			
25	Mergers and Acquisitions			
	Do you have any acquisitions for happiness?			
	What are they?			
	What should they be?			

26	Co-opetition			
	Do you have a Co-opetition strategy for happiness?			
	What is it?			
	What should it be?			
27	Blue Ocean Strategy			
	Do you have a Blue Ocean strategy for happiness?			
	What is it?			
	What should it be?			

<table>
<tr><td rowspan="4">28</td><td colspan="4">Business Model</td></tr>
<tr><td>Do you have a business model for happiness?</td><td></td><td></td><td></td></tr>
<tr><td colspan="4">What is it?</td></tr>
<tr><td colspan="4">What should it be?</td></tr>
<tr><td rowspan="4">29</td><td colspan="4">Strategy Execution</td></tr>
<tr><td>Do you have an execution strategy for happiness?</td><td></td><td></td><td></td></tr>
<tr><td colspan="4">What is it?</td></tr>
<tr><td colspan="4">What should it be?</td></tr>
</table>

<table>
<tr><td rowspan="4">30</td><td colspan="4">Resource Allocation</td></tr>
<tr><td>Have you done resource allocation for happiness?</td><td></td><td></td><td></td></tr>
<tr><td colspan="4">How are you ensuring proper resource allocation?</td></tr>
<tr><td colspan="4">What should you do to improve it further?</td></tr>
<tr><td rowspan="4">31</td><td colspan="4">Growth Trap</td></tr>
<tr><td>Have you fallen into growth trap?</td><td></td><td></td><td></td></tr>
<tr><td colspan="4">How are you ensuring avoiding the growth trap?</td></tr>
<tr><td colspan="4">How should you avoid it?</td></tr>
</table>

<table>
<tr><td rowspan="4">32</td><td colspan="4">Focus & Discipline</td></tr>
<tr><td>Are you staying focused on your strategy?</td><td></td><td></td><td></td></tr>
<tr><td colspan="4">How are you ensuring the discipline and focus on the strategy?</td></tr>
<tr><td colspan="4">How you should do it?</td></tr>
<tr><td rowspan="4">33</td><td colspan="4">Execution Troubles</td></tr>
<tr><td colspan="4">What are your execution issues?</td></tr>
<tr><td colspan="4">How are you solving these issues?</td></tr>
<tr><td colspan="4">How you should do it?</td></tr>
</table>

34	Curse of Knowledge			
	Are you facing curse of knowledge situation for your happiness strategy?			
	How are you avoiding it?			
	How should you improve it further?			
35	Importance of Assumptions			
	What are your assumptions for happiness?			
	Are they correct?			
	Do you keep checking your assumption about happiness?			
36	Paralysis by Analysis			
	Have you faced paralysis by analysis?			
	How are you taking care of it?			
	How you should take care of it?			

<table>
<tr><td rowspan="4">37</td><td colspan="4">Platform Strategy</td></tr>
<tr><td colspan="4">What is your platform strategy for happiness?</td></tr>
<tr><td colspan="4">Is it correct?</td></tr>
<tr><td colspan="4">What it should be?</td></tr>
<tr><td rowspan="4">38</td><td colspan="4">Strategic Alignment</td></tr>
<tr><td>Are your activities aligned with your happiness story?</td><td></td><td></td><td></td></tr>
<tr><td colspan="4">What are you doing for the strategic alignment?</td></tr>
<tr><td colspan="4">What you should be doing for it?</td></tr>
<tr><td rowspan="4">39</td><td colspan="4">Entrepreneurship</td></tr>
<tr><td>Do you have an entrepreneurship strategy for happiness?</td><td></td><td></td><td></td></tr>
<tr><td colspan="4">What is it?</td></tr>
<tr><td colspan="4">What should it be?</td></tr>
</table>

40	Innovation			
	Do you have an innovation strategy for happiness?			
	What is it?			
	What should it be?			
41	International Strategy			
	Do you have an international strategy for happiness?			
	What is it?			
	What should it be?			
42	Transnational Model			
	Do you have a transnational strategy for happiness?			
	What is it?			
	What should it be?			

<table>
<tr><td rowspan="4">43</td><td colspan="4">Corporate Governance</td></tr>
<tr><td>Do you have corporate governance strategy for happiness?</td><td></td><td></td><td></td></tr>
<tr><td colspan="4">What is it?</td></tr>
<tr><td colspan="4">What should it be?</td></tr>
<tr><td rowspan="4">44</td><td colspan="4">Strategic Corporate Social Responsibility (CSR)</td></tr>
<tr><td>Do you have a strategic CSR for happiness?</td><td></td><td></td><td></td></tr>
<tr><td colspan="4">What is it?</td></tr>
<tr><td colspan="4">What should it be?</td></tr>
<tr><td rowspan="4">45</td><td colspan="4">Organizational Structure</td></tr>
<tr><td>Do you have an organizational structure for happiness?</td><td></td><td></td><td></td></tr>
<tr><td colspan="4">What is it?</td></tr>
<tr><td colspan="4">What should it be?</td></tr>
</table>

<table>
<tr><td rowspan="4">46</td><td colspan="4">McKinsey 7S Framework</td></tr>
<tr><td>Do you have a McKinsey 7S framework for happiness?</td><td></td><td></td><td></td></tr>
<tr><td colspan="4">What is it?</td></tr>
<tr><td colspan="4">What should it be?</td></tr>
<tr><td rowspan="4">47</td><td colspan="4">Emergent Strategy</td></tr>
<tr><td>Do you have an emergent strategy for happiness?</td><td></td><td></td><td></td></tr>
<tr><td colspan="4">How your strategy for happiness has emerged?</td></tr>
<tr><td colspan="4">How should it have emerged?</td></tr>
</table>

<table>
<tr><td rowspan="4">48</td><td colspan="4">Balanced Scorecard</td></tr>
<tr><td>Do you have a balance score-card for happiness?</td><td></td><td></td><td></td></tr>
<tr><td colspan="4">What is it?</td></tr>
<tr><td colspan="4">What should it be?</td></tr>
</table>

49	Limitations of Strategy			
	Are you aware of limitations of your strategy for happiness?			
	How are you managing it?			
	How should you manage it?			

Annexure VI

Further Free Sources on Strategy

- Free membership websites for latest articles on strategy.

  http://knowledge.wharton.upenn.edu/
  https://sloanreview.mit.edu/
  https://cmr.berkeley.edu/blog/
  https://hbr.org/topic/strategy
  https://www.mckinsey.com/quarterly/
  https://www.bcgperspectives.com/

- There are free videos on YouTube by leading thinkers in strategy. You can easily find it through google search. E.g. https://www.youtube.com/user/HarvardBSchool/videos
- There are number of courses on strategy available for free on MIT OpenCourseWare and similar platforms. You can easily find it through google search. E.g. https://ocw.mit.edu/index.htm
- For a humorous perspective on strategy and innovation, visit www. pillania.org and watch YouTube channel of Prof Rajesh Pillania

Brief Profile Of The Author

Dr. Rajesh K Pillania is rated and awarded the Top Professor of Strategy in India by ASSOCHAM and Education Post. He is ranked jointly number one in average research productivity among management faculty (including IIMs/IITs) in India for research output from 1968 to 2014 [By Prof Ramdhar Singh of IIM Banglore and others in 2015 which was published in a reputed international journal titled Omega in 2017]. He is on the advisory board of many esteemed international research journals, professional bodies and conferences consisting of leading international academicians, industry leaders and policy makers.

He is passionate about strategy and his areas of expertise are strategy, innovation strategy, strategy in India, global strategy, demystifying strategy, strategic humour and happiness strategy. His research is focused on two broad areas. First one is on the frontiers of strategic management and second one is on democratizing strategy. For frontiers of strategic management, he is involved with a number of esteemed international research journals and has written research papers and books. For democratizing strategy, he has published innovative humourous books which are available on Amazon, offers strategy workshops, and writes on strategy in popular media such as Times of India and The Economic Times, etc.

Besides being a prolific writer and a popular teacher; he has conducted various executive development programs for middle to senior management and, has conducted consulting assignments for top management of organizations. He is Professor of Strategy with MDI Gurgaon and holds a Ph.D in Strategy. His academic and research experience includes University Business School, Panjab University (Chandigarh, India); Management Development Institute (Gurgaon, India); Indian Institute of Management Kozhikode (Kozhikode, India); R. H. Smith School of Business, University of Maryland (Maryland, USA); Harvard University (Boston, USA); and MCI Management Centre (Innsbruck, Austria) among others.

For more, please visit www. pillania.org and he can be reached at rajesh@pillania.org

Executive Development Programs/ Training

Some of the training programs offered by Prof Rajesh Pillania are given below.

- Strategic Humour: Strategy Made Easy for All
- Innovation Humour: Innovation Made Easy for All.
- Happiness Strategy: Happiness Made Easy for All.
- Strategy for High Performance
- Innovations for High Performance
- Strategy with Intuition
- Disruptive Strategy
- Humour for All
- Key MBA Learnings for All.

For more, please visit www.pillania.org and he can be reached at rajesh@pillania.org